ALASKAN LONELY HEARTS CLUB

T0346964

ALASKAN LONELY HEARTS CLUB

HEARTS CLUB

And Other Unlikely Travel Tales

PAUL GOGARTY

ILLUSTRATIONS BY DAVID ABSE

Signal

Signal Books

Oxford

First published in 2017 by
Signal Books Limited
36 Minster Road
Oxford OX4 1LY
www.signalbooks.co.uk

© Paul Gogarty, 2017
Illustrations © David Abse

A catalogue record for this book is available from the British Library

ISBN 978-1-909930-54-4 Paper

Cover Design: Tora Kelly
Production: Tora Kelly
Cover Images: David Abse
Printed in India by Imprint Digital

TO SUSANNA, LARNE AND MAX AS ALWAYS

CONTENTS

FOREWORD BY NICHOLAS CRANE

We bonded in Alice Springs. A wartime, twin-prop DC-3 had ferried us across the Simpson Desert at flak-altitude. I remember a river with no water and turbulence butting the venerable old fuselage. Paul spent the flight taking notes. We were in Australia for less than a week and he had managed to scoop no fewer than five commissions for British newspapers and magazines. I had one commission. We landed late in the day but Paul still had time to meet an Aboriginal Australian who shared his life story and taught him the rudiments of boomerang-throwing. By nightfall, Paul had a sixth commission. I have never travelled with a writer more tuned to story-telling. It's not a common aptitude. Sensory antennae have to be perpetually alert for cultural curiosities; for strange sights, sounds and smells; for strangers with time to talk; for half-open doors in unfamiliar places. It needs confidence and humility. I learned a lot on that trip.

Great travel writing takes the reader beyond their own borders. I luxuriate in the lines of this book because I couldn't have written them. All stories rise from the unique wellsprings of their authors and Paul's come from Liverpool and Ireland, from music and poetry and literature and from a fascination with the foibles of humankind. Who but Paul would describe Irish hills "zippered with grey stone walls"? Hemingway, Camus and Kesey share these pages with Sadashiva Yogi and Stella from Bromsgrove. We ride a train across Alaska, a horse over the Burren and a two-tone Harley Softail Classic along Highway 1. These alphabet-episodes take us to places on planets apart: a holiday centre in Great Yarmouth and Tootsie's Orchid Lounge in Nashville; Funzi Island (it's south of Mombasa) and Ilulissat, a town in Greenland where sledge dogs outnumber humans. But it's dialogue that lifts humanity from the page and this book has a cast of hundreds, from Ed, the druidical Cornishman who'd seen angels landing on his 18-ton, homemade dolmen, to Krystal the barmaid in Talkeetna who produced a line too priceless to be spoiled in a Foreword. It is part of Paul's craft to recognise that the world is not gifted with a restricted supply of "characters" who might be persuaded to share their 24-carat stories with word-prospectors from foreign lands. In Paul's world, everybody has a story. Alchemy is wrought in the transcription.

Never has it mattered more to engage with the geographies of this incredible planet. In an era of accelerated habitat change, old landscapes are losing colour and accessibility. Like a box of 35mm slides left in the loft, treasured places fade and become more difficult to find. Travel writers have always been the counterforce, revealing new places and reviving old ones; returning home with a fresh crop of anecdote and insight that puts colour back in the cheeks of armchair adventurers. And these days, travel writing has a supernumerary role in the fight against the prejudice and fear being constructed by those who'd have us believe in a future of isolationism. I hope you enjoy this book as much as I have.

INTRODUCTION

As a child conscript following my father round his army postings I never lived anywhere more than three years as we transitted through Streatham, Shropshire, Wiltshire, Malaysia, Hong Kong, Liverpool, Hampshire, Germany and Pembrokeshire. As soon as I hit sixteen, I quit home in a hurry and got a job as an unmoored deck hand ferrying tourists from the Welsh coastal resort of Tenby across to the holy island of Caldey.

A year later I was kicking my heels in London, temping, making tea for men in stained grey suits and making no sense of the cabalistic arts of advertising nor quantity surveying, nor the machinations at County Hall. When, at nineteen, I moved out to Spain to a job in a bar on the Costa Dorada, it felt a much better nomadic fit which led to me taking up English teaching posts in Algeria, Cyprus and Japan through my twenties. Then I became a travel writer and made life on the road my fixed state.

Travelling the planet I've encountered shakers, fakers and wilderness women as well as high-heeled naked yogis and low-slung hawkers selling everything from a toe nail of St Xavier to a frying pan embossed with an image of St Bernadette.

In Alaska - at the heart of Wrangell-St Elias National Park (the size of Yellowstone, Yosemite and Switzerland combined) - I was once cooked a five-course meal by a cage-fighting chef named Joshua Slaughter. At Victoria Falls a witchdoctor scattered bones in the dust and then peered long and hard before declaring I'd never marry - "Never, never, never." When I told him I already was and had two children, unabashed he quickly added, "Again; I said you'll never marry again."

Then there were the trips that led straight to hospital including flying off a sand dune in a buggy on California's Pismo Beach (ten stitches over the right eye) and being smashed in the head by a careering metal ski-lift casement in the Alps (twelve stitches over the left eye). There were arrests too, such as when I found myself surrounded by a dozen machine-gun toting officers at Hong Kong airport (a US cartridge-case souvenir of mine from Vietnam had sent airport security into meltdown).

In Rome I was taught the art of gladiatorial combat by a Scotsman and in Canada instructed in the art of mushing by a guesthouse owner who confessed to hating people - "all people; no exceptions". In Australia's outback I was tutored in the art of boomerang throwing by an Aboriginal ex-professional boxer forcibly separated from his twin sister and mother at the age of six (when the

Japanese bombed his orphanage, he led thirty fellow orphans on a three-month walkabout). And yes, in Korea I was once gunned down in an oil-drum garage diner.

*

Parts of some of these stories have appeared previously in the *Daily Telegraph*, *Guardian*, *Times*, *Sunday Times*, *Daily Mail*, *Independent* and *Observer*.

ALASKAN BACHELOR AUCTION

Female US Air Force sergeant seeks genuine wilderness man

'm still in my thermals and out for the count when the bell clangs up at th railroad crossing. Somewhere deep inside my hangover I realise with horro that the once-a-day train to Anchorage is about to pull in. Hitting panic mod I whirl round the cabin like a dervish throwing on clothes and fur-lined boo and am about to charge out of the door when I notice I've somehow missed m trousers.

Eventually I emerge from the cabin into deep snow drifts. The yellow Alask State Railroad sign above the open freight door seems impossibly distant but somehow make it and launch my bag up into the wagon. A handsome ebon giant in the peak cap and smart blue railroad uniform of a thousand movie holds out his hand and yanks me on board with a smile. He is the first black ma I've seen in this white wilderness state the size of Western Europe.

The door slams and the train pulls out and I make my way to a passenge carriage. Over the next four hours we shuffle south between spindly blac forests and endless white Saharas - the next town with real roads due west is S Petersburg, just under 4,000 miles away.

There are two others seated in the passenger carriage. One, a plump youn girl with acne, I recall from the previous night's Bachelor Auction when I' watched in disbelief as a hirsute male, naked apart from a beaver G string danced and fondled his way between the rows of packed women, his scrotu swinging freely beneath his loose-fitting thong. The second passenger, a male is staring at a magazine called *Alaska Men*, a monthly lonely hearts that sells t women in their thousands throughout the United States (and reputedly to jus as many men).

The man introduces himself as Brad and pushes the folded magazin across. "That's me." He points to a dog-eared page which shows hin squatting in a forest, stroking an Alsatian. Accompanying the photograph i a profile that informs prospective suitors of Brad's passion for the wildernes and skijoring (being pulled on skis by huskies), and warns that he seek "friendship first before getting serious". Other entries from rather fe frontiersmen veer from the bizarre to the endearing – "Kenneth enjoys scub diving, dancing and cooking, and he also lists 'kissing' as one of his favourit things."

The issue is three months old and Brad has been carrying it round lik a rosary since it first hit the newsstands. "Got over 100 replies from lonel women in every corner of the Lower 48," he brags. The Lower 48 by the way i how Alaskans refer to America's other 48 mainland states. "Some women eve visited," Brad continues and then adds, somewhat crestfallen, "but none hung around for some reason." A Californian woman from the Lower 48 interviewe by CBS at Anchorage airport after a recent unsuccessful bachelor prospecting rip probably had Brad's answer. When asked what she thought of Alaskan matrimonial prospects, she replied, "Well … the odds are good. But the goods are odddddd."

The Wilderness Women Competition and the Bachelor Auction I'd just attended in Talkeetna had definitely been the ultimate expression of such Alaskan oddness but my winter oddity had actually started a week earlier in the capital, Anchorage.

Alaska is a rufty-tufty, outdoorsy, frontiersy kind of place where men are men and so are the women. With wraparound snow vistas and days cut to a few hours in mid-winter, it can feel like you're inhabiting a deep freeze, which is exactly what you are. Outsiders may believe the whole state locks itself away shellacking frozen moose droppings through the winter for when the tourists arrive but in reality Alaskans, enjoying a balmy -15°C to - 40°C, will be out mushing over iced rivers, spinning light aircraft over hanging glaciers, snowmobiling, climbing frozen waterfalls and fishing through ice holes. Their philosophy is simple: wrap up, get out, enjoy. And, if the weather turns really nasty, Alaskans are really good at getting drunk.

When I first hit Anchorage it was midnight but I was on 9am; day was night for me and pretty much for them too with darkness falling around 3pm and lying in till gone 10 the next morning.

My 17th floor hotel room looked out over a low-slung, gridded city. Streets were compacted snow and more of the white stuff was still falling. Car headlights groped through the opaline night, tyres crunching new tracks, street lights pulsing like coals in a grate, and chiffons of smoke drifted across a starless sky. I was spent but before turning in, I put in an "Aurora Wake Up Call" - if the Northern Lights did put in an appearance, I wasn't going to miss it.

The next morning, just a three-minute walk from my hotel, I stood looking south over the frozen mudrocks of the Cook Inlet to humpbacked Mount Susitna. Wind gnawed at any exposed flesh and snow swirled off rooftops. Hungry ravens squawked their raucous disputations above office workers langlaufing their way into work along the ten-mile coastal trail. Walking up 9th Avenue I passed a moose caught up in Christmas lights decorating a spruce tree. In someone's backyard I saw a reindeer kept as a pet and about to be taken for its daily walk along 10th Avenue. Instead of civic notables, the only bronze statue in town was of a husky signalling the starting line of "the world's last great race" - the 1,000-mile Iditarod. At the Oomingmak Shop I stroked shawls and mittens woven by Eskimos from the under hair of the primeval musk oxen. At the Anchorage Historical and Fine Arts Museum, I marvelled at a cribbage board carved from walrus ivory, a coat made of cormorant pelts, a belt made of caribou teeth, and mukluks (boots) made from transparent fish skins.

That night I trawled the bars which, like the restaurants, were dressed with identical stuffed moose and grizzlies as well as the carcasses of 300-pound halibuts and fifty-pound salmon. As I sat in one bar, a hat rack belonging to a moose passed the window. At Fly by Night, a 1980s Miss Alaska by the name of Alice Wellings got into her act, seductively pacing herself through her put-on rather than strip-off, routine. This climaxed with her grinning, fully clothed in hip waders and a halibut wool coat as the crowd clapped and bayed "Put 'em on, put 'em on!"

Those inhabiting the bush disparagingly say that Anchorage is only thirty minutes from Alaska so the next morning, just before catching the train for Talkeetna, I took a drive out in a hire car along Northern Lights Avenue which feeds onto Seward Highway. On my right, the second highest tide in the world was on its way out, seeking a route through clumps of frozen mud and ice as snow swirled like smoke across the road.

As I rounded a bend, I noticed an overturned car in a pillow of snow steaming like an exhausted husky. A door opened heavenward. I pulled over and, with snow up to my knees, helped the driver get his two young daughters and wife out. When I asked if they were ok, the driver replied as laconically as if he'd just pulled into a supermarket parking lot, "Sure buddy, snow's good for flipping in."

It was time to drive back into town and catch the train to Talkeetna, the strangest place of all in this strangest of states.

Most communities grow up at crossroads. But in Talkeetna it is the end of the road that people seek. The railroad came in 1923; the road came, and expired only in 1965. This town of some 736 very scattered souls is located where three major rivers, the Talkeetna, the Susitna and the Chulitna, run through steep cuts creating staggeringly beautiful valleys and views out to the Alaska Range and North America's highest peak, Mount McKinley.

"Town" consists of a post office, a school, three bars, three restaurants and two general stores - one of which doubles up as the single-pump gas station. And like every other town in Alaska, there's also an airstrip (from which pioneering bush pilot, Don Sheldon, reputedly managed to crash 26 times without loss of life).

Talkeetna grew up at the turn of the century as a supply point for prospectors and hunters who'd visit, in the words of trapper Gary Hermes, "to get drunk, get laid, get a haircut and provisions". The perennial problem for wilderness man then as now, however, was finding a woman willing to share the wilderness with. To scrape a living, Gary sometimes opened his shop, The Dutchman's Gunsmith, and sometimes he didn't, preferring to head out gold prospecting or hunting "like the old buckskinners with just a single-shot flint or cap-and-ball rifle".

In 1980, as the gold miners, oil men, mountain guides, flightseeing pilots, construction workers, fishermen and trappers endured another eighteen-hour night in the Fairview Inn, the oldest bar in town, someone hit upon an idea for luring women in. They would hold an all-day wilderness-women competition with tests of strength, agility and servitude; and follow it up with a Bachelor Auction and Ball in the evening. Not many women stuck around long but everybody had such a good time that it became a December fixture.

The current bash had drawn a smattering of out-of-towners including me. It seemed only right that I should start by paying my respects where the weekend had been dreamt up, in the Fairview, but as I rounded the corner on treacherous ice, my stay almost came to a premature end as a skidoo missed me by inches.

Inside the inn, a sign requested, "All firearms must be checked with the bartender before ordering drinks." A second demanded, "Dog teams must be tied away from the inn." A line of hunched plaid shirts and baseball caps sat round a horseshoe bar drinking rum and Alaska Amber beneath moose and caribou antlers, bear skins, a mural of Mount McKinley and Xmas fairy lights. A few tables had been pushed to the walls leaving the well-worn wooden dance floor free for anyone suffering SAD (Seasonal Affective Disorder or cabin fever). According to the barman, the quickest cure, "apart from a plane ride to Hawaii", was "to swirl around the dance floor with a bottle of rum inside you".

Having got myself a beer, I pulled up a chair at a table in the back room where married, retired oilman Harold Heinze was helping three younger men from the Bachelor Society paste members' photographs into a catalogue that was to be given out to the hopefully packed female bidders at tomorrow night's meat market. Reading one of the "Bachelor Biographies", I learned that the most exciting moment in Joe Watson's life had been "Driving a Cat" - a truck sized-sledge pulled by Caterpillar trucks to and from mining areas. Under "What do you do for entertainment?" Joe had answered, "Work," and what he was looking for in a woman was "A good heart".

Soon I was roped in to replace Harold who had to leave abruptly when a message came over the community radio informing him his wife had flipped the truck into a ditch on the way home after too many drinks. It could have been worse - she might have run into a 1,000lb moose. Or a bear. Not so long ago on another dark night after parking her car, she'd apparently walked straight into the waist of one.

As Harold left, Joe Kirwin, the Society's president, shook his head wistfully: "See that's what we're missin' - havin' someone to pull out a ditch." Dick Smith, a workmate in the same heavy equipment company, said nothing. He no doubt was mentally choreographing his beaver G-string dance for the next evening.

Krystal Henson, a barmaid at Latitude 62, a bar located on the other side of the railway track, complained that would-be romantic knights like Joe were thin on the ground. "The reason there are so many bachelors in Talkeetna is choice ... women's choice. Half ain't fit to marry and the other half already are... You know what Talkeetna men use for contraception?" Krystal didn't wait for an answer. "Their personalities." To prove her point she cited the case of Chicken Pete who put himself up for auction each year and had only been bought once - for $30. "Who wants to buy a man who has a chicken for a girlfriend and is always kissin' and cuddlin' the raggedy ol' thing in the front cab of his truck?" Another bachelor taking his date back to his cabin in the bush on his skidoo the year before had hit some thin ice and sunk into the river. "Were they alright? Did he manage to save his date?" I asked. "Heck no, he was too busy savin' his skidoo. She had to walk back to town herself frozen like moose nuggets."

Krystal, who'd already won the Wilderness Women competition twice, would not be entering this year. She'd decided to give the younger girls a chance. From Latitude 62, a flame-haired 24-year-old fellow barmaid, Heather McIntyre, would be competing. I told her I'd be rooting for her.

Gary Hermes, a 54-year-old ZZ Top lookalike with beard flowing all the way to his prodigious dungareed girth, similarly was thinking of cancelling his registration for auction this year. "Been married four times and enough's enough." The longest a woman had stuck his 12' x 16' cabin four miles from town was eighteen months. "Ain't none of 'em prepared to run to the outhouse through five to eight feet of snow nor fetch five-gallon bottles of water from town when it's minus thirty... I guess they're just spoilt these days."

The temperature by noon the following morning was five degrees ("a scorcher," one competitor told me, "last year it was minus twenty"). Outside my cabin, I could see five-foot, wind-sculpted snow drifts and female contestants preparing for those tests of strength, agility and servitude. They would be outdoors in the freezing weather for the best part of three hours.

In the first event, designed to cut the field down to five, twenty contestants raced against the clock carrying two five-gallon containers of water 200 yards down Main Street and back again over icy compacted snow. Heather from Latitude 62 didn't make the cut but was philosophical. "Guess smoking and drinking ain't the best trainin' for this event." In the next event, the five remaining contestants had to carry a sandwich and drink across the ice to a bachelor sitting in front of a TV tuned to the National Football League. Clearly the women were not so keen on the servitude bit and most took the opportunity to throw the food and drink over the men. Having unloaded the refreshments, they then had to load logs into a sledge and pull it behind a skidoo before unloading them onto a fire. The fastest time won.

In between events the crowd of no more than sixty warmed their rears over the fire, popped into Nagley's store for half bottles of whisky and bagels, or drifted into the Fairview for hot chocolate, rum and more beers. Gary from ZZ Top was helping out with events dressed only in a plaid shirt and his dungarees; out-of-towners like me wore fifteen layers and still shivered.

The final event involved putting on snow shoes and scooting across a simulated hunt course that required contestants to track a moose, shoot, ptarmigan and snare a foam fish. The eventual winner, Erica, also had to contend with locating a contact lens she'd dropped in the snow which she subsequently popped into her mouth for safe keeping while she finished the course. Resourceful. She would be crowned and presented with two air tickets to anywhere in the United States at the ball that evening. She said she'd probably take her mum to Florida.

The crowd broke up, dogs yapped excitedly from Dodge and Ford pickups as their masters returned, skidoos revved and Talkeetners returned to their cabins to prepare for the evening revel. I instead headed out for a little mushing in the valley with a team of eight dogs that pulled me across the milky desert. It was 2.30pm and the sun already fanned its goodbye in gold bars over Mount McKinley. The dogs yelped, I yelped with them and returned to my cabin as frozen as Krystal's moose nuggets.

That evening I walked gingerly on frozen Main Street past wooden cabins engulfed in their white dreamy drifts, December's darkness softened by garlands of Christmas lights. Eventually I found the Tee Pee, an A-frame timber building containing both a bar and a hall in which the auction and ball would be held.

Sixty metal school chairs had already been nabbed. The only males present, apart from me and a couple of other voyeurs who'd paid $100 to a local charity to attend, were those on sale. The air throbbed with the sexual frisson of an Ann Summers party. Heavy coats and boots had been sloughed, hair was being brushed through a final time and earrings adjusted.

A local bachelor and amateur country-and-western singer innocently announced, "I've been sent out to warm you up," and was drowned beneath wolf whistles. If the women had their way I have little doubt the cowboy on stage would have performed an Alaskan Full Monty. Manfully he struggled through three songs which everybody in the audience, except me, seemed to know the words to, before a butch female MC next commenced a lewd barrage of sexual slights on Talkeetna males. Significantly, however, when she asked, "How many of you out there has had a real date in the last three years?", only three hands went up. A palpable nervousness could be detected beneath the women's macho exterior that I suspected hid a genuine hope that tonight might be the night they finally found a mate.

One by one a motley, hirsute crew were brought on stage and introduced to more wolf whistles. The meat market began. Bids were made: those ready for the knacker's yard going for $30, other prime beasts encouraging more robust bidding. All the successful claimant was guaranteed was a rose, a drink, a dance and a date and yet there was a frenzy to proceedings now. A female sergeant stationed at a nearby US Air Force base, who had tried to calm her nerves with several rums, found she had bought three bachelors when bidding closed. When the aptly named Dick Smith, eyes on stalks and scrotum swinging, danced his way down the aisles to a J. Geils Band track that seemed to be on a constant loop, he amused and terrified the audience but unsurprisingly only got one bid for a measly $30.

The top two studs both went for $130: Greg was a protean Alaskan Neanderthal and geologist, Henry a fifty-year-old university lecturer and annual musher in the Iditirod. ZZ Gary, who'd decided to enter after all, had been stunned to fetch $50 - "the most I ever went for" - and was still dancing with potential Wilderness Woman number five when I left for the Fairview to catch the second set of an old-school R'n B band from Anchorage who for some reason had christened themselves Texas Lightning.

Many of the same faces from the auction were on the floor dancing extravagantly when I arrived soon after 11pm. For a while I stood discussing with Don, the 65-year-old bar owner, his second retirement plan (the Fairview had been his first) and chatting with Chip, a mountain guide who'd spent twelve years climbing the Alaska Range but "I still can't manage to tame my wife." Eventually, however, the band had everyone on the floor. The good mood that had been building all day was at the wonderfully out-of-control, seriously drunk stage. Winter cabin fever had been seen off for another few weeks.

Around 3am I realised I hadn't eaten and popped across for the "all-night breakfast" being served at the Roadhouse. More than anywhere else in town the Roadhouse was where alternative met wilderness, granola met reindeer sausage, longhaired-mountaineer-in-Peruvian-jumper met authors-in-plaid-shirts and construction workers in Cat boots. As I attempted to stem the slide to hangover with coffee, Gary arrived with his new bride and a smile as long as the Yukon River. I headed for bed and my Alaskan Railway wake-up call.

BLACK SHEEP

My famous Irish relly

The sun shone. Telephone wires loped between bleached pine poles across the bog to slate-grey mountains. A mile ahead of me, a lone car snaked its way past a lake which appeared to have taken a great sigh and spilled across the skinny road. Above it, from fissures in the green hills, streams of dark water tumbled, transformed into white foam. I've discovered many memorable landscapes in Ireland - the haunting peninsulas of West Cork, the Kerrygold green of Killarney's lakeland, the ethereal beauty of Lough Derg - but none can hold a light to Connemara.

I'd first been exposed to its wild beauty eighteen months earlier on a fleeting visit when, filling in the car-hire form at Shannon airport, the agent - clearly concerned about her spelling acumen — reduced my wife's stated occupation of psychotherapist to "psycho". I continue to remind her of it whenever we have a row. On our late Sunday dash back to the airport from Clifden, we'd noticed a sign to Renvyle House Hotel off the main Galway road. Could it be the same Renvyle that had been home to poet, senator surgeon, "wildest wit in Dublin" (George William Russell) and highly tenuous relative Oliver St. John Gogarty?

Fortunately there was no time to find out. I say fortunately because I'd long claimed Gogarty as family on the evidence of a shared surname and someone in a pub once telling my father he was his spitting image. Dad had always been vague about his Irish ancestry - his own father, Charles, was born in London to a Dubliner by the name of Mary Gogarty. Like Oliver, Charles had been dead more than forty years, and I was happy to let sleeping dogs lie. Any light shone on the matter would almost inevitably banish me to the darkness of familial obscurity. Someone who drove a buttercup-yellow Rolls Royce (Ireland's first Rolls), who'd removed W.B. Yeats' tonsils (whose gratitude no doubt explained his declaration of Gogarty as "one of the greatest lyric poets of the age"), fired a revolver over the head of James Joyce, provided secret refuge for Republican Michael Collins before his assassination, and dived into the frozen waters of the Liffey to escape his own Republican firing squad, was clearly worth hanging onto, however tenuously.

Unknown to me, however, a less timid cousin and an aunt had been doing research which suggested that Oliver, remarkably, could really be related. They believed Oliver's sister Mary (also known as Mayflo) had run off with an impecunious writer to London where she gave birth to Charles. The writer did a bunk, Mayflo abandoned her son and married a Harley Street doctor. When Dr Roden Ryan in turn died, Mayflo moved to Hollywood to join other relatives My own grandfather, Charles, meanwhile, grew up with someone he called "Grandmother" and eventually fathered four children of his own, one of whom was my father (also called Charles).

Birth and death certificates still had to be found for official verification but as far as I was concerned I could now start strutting. I therefore planned a hasty return to the source of the diaspora, now directly related and, even better, on the black-sheep side of the family.

Re-reading Ulick O'Connor's wonderful hagiography of Gogarty, I discovered that the hotel I'd seen signposted in Connemara was indeed the poet's "sea-grey house". Gogarty, strapped for cash, had converted his home into a hotel in 1930 and it had remained that way after the family sold it on to another Connemara family in 1952. I booked a family room and confirmation duly arrived along with a copy of *A Sea-Grey House: the History of Renvyle House* by Guy St. John Williams. The author, I read, was Gogarty's grandson and he lived two miles from Renvyle on Heather Island where Oliver had relocated when Renvyle became a hotel.

Before leaving home, I dropped Guy a letter to tell him the Muswell Hill branch of the Gogarty clan was descending on Connemara and that I hoped we'd be able to meet up.

At the head of a lough, incandescent in the sun, a stone bridge framed the knuckled spine of the Twelve Bens. Bog lawns, dotted with lichen-stained rocks and bog asphodels, erupted in hummocks of deer grass. In the lee of an outcrop overlooking the road, a lone whitewashed cottage perched like a sea eagle. We drove on past the gentle pale crenellations of Kylemore Abbey and an explosion of rhododendron and wild fuchsia until we reached a drive that led to Gogarty's "long, long house in the ultimate land of the undiscovered West ... where islands and mountainous mainland share in a final reconciliation at this, the world's end."

The slate-walled house stood "on the edge of the sea on the last shelf of Europe in the next parish to New York". It floated in a sorcerer's ether that had guests talking to each other the moment they arrived, seduced palms into believing they were growing in Florida, and magically kept a freshwater lake separate from the ocean by the merest rumour of land. On the pebbled seashore, black-tarred currachs lay beached like seals and beyond them a hundred phantom islands dotted the bay. It felt like we'd crossed into the fairy isles.

Gogarty had bought Renvyle as a retreat in 1917 but talk for Gogarty was what dance was to the Dervishes and he ended up taking Dublin society with him. Gogarty at Renvyle, as in Dublin, was no less the Irish Literary Renaissance's master of ceremonies than Beau Nash had been in Georgian Bath. (Dublin's Artists, painters and politicians had two options when they wanted a break: they either headed to Lady Gregory's Coole Park or a little further north to Gogarty's Renvyle.)

Although Gogarty had sold the hotel forty years earlier, the present owners still celebrated the man. A plaque outside commemorated his life and a fine bronze bust of Gogarty took pride of place in the lobby where voices were soft Dublin or Galwegian with a smattering of plummy Anglo calling from the deep sofas like Sirens. Framed on walls or clearly visible beneath table glass like pressed butterflies were the letters, telegrams, theatre notices and drafts of poems of Gogarty's life. The bar still had room enough for dancing during the spontaneous sessions that erupted each night and wisely the owners had retained large indefinable spaces that served no other purpose than socialising in Gogarty's time and which any modern hotelier worth his salt would long since have carved into another ten bedrooms. The billiard room invited shared intimacies, and the large library upstairs offered conversations with Swift, Wilde and Joyce. Once a week, instead of the karaoke or bingo favoured by other hotels, a play was staged for the edification of guests on the life of both Gogarty and Renvyle.

Out on the beach, children were skimming stones towards rust-coloured islands, their parents having disappeared onto the nine-hole golf course or into the bar. Within the hotel grounds younger kids wielded croquet sticks taller than themselves or participated with gusto in a pell-mell mixed-sex football match. My son Max, aged seven at the time, was among the latter. Larne, then aged ten, had already disappeared to the stables "to help out".

At 9.30pm, about the time Augustus John, Gogarty, Cosgrave and Yeats would have been heading into the Library with their post-prandials, the children were flocking to the open-air pool where a rubber cover had been partially pulled across the water so that they could pretend they were walking across a bog. Indoors, peat fires smouldered in grates just as they did in Gogarty's time and a waitress was ferrying Marmite sandwiches and hot milk upstairs for smaller sprogs who had earlier curfews.

Early the next morning the telephone rang. An unfamiliar voice greeted me, "Good morning cousin." It was Guy St. John Williams, Oliver's grandson and author of *A Sea-Grey House*. We followed his directions passing "through the farmer's gate on a track over a hill down to Tully Lake", arriving on the dot at 10am. From the dense vegetation of Heather Island, I made out a checked shirt-sleeve waving to us and two dogs jumping up and down excitedly. As Guy rowed across the still water, dispensing welcomes as he approached the stone jetty, I surreptitiously viewed him: the blue eyes were decidedly mine and the high forehead, but triumphantly I noticed that England's kinder climate had been more follicle-friendly to me. On the minus side, Guy was wirier; my own frame edging ominously towards his grandfather, "Stately plump Buck Mulligan" (as Gogarty was immortalised by Joyce in *Ulysses*).

Guy rowed us back to his nine-acre island where the dogs, Teal and Plover, yapped wildly in anticipation of new playmates. We followed them through the undergrowth, skirting a circle of rowan trees ("to keep the fairies out") and a small orchard planted by the Seventh Duke of Leinster in the late 1930s: "He could stick Heather Island no better than he could his wives - six of them he went through and four bankruptcies."

Hidden among the verdant vegetation was another long house which had only just got electricity and a phone but still had water pumping directly from the lake into its taps. My children took off with the two dogs to explore the island. All bar one of Guy's own five children were absent and she, like any self-respecting teenager, was still in bed.

The house's lack of natural light, plentiful nooks and crannies, low beams, dormer windows and steep gables lent credence to the rumour that Lutyens had had something to do with its construction. A series of small rooms were littered with the detritus of Guy's dual careers as a writer and jockey/trainer/club official. Hung on one wall was a copy of a portrait of Guy's mother (and Oliver's daughter), the sculptress Brenda Gogarty, painted by Augustus John. A bust by Brenda of Jack Yeats (a.k.a W.B) stood on a desk beside a draft of a poem Guy had been working on ("I'm an occasional poet - I only write poems when I'm drunk"). There was also a handgun. I wondered if it was the one Oliver had fired over James Joyce's head when they lived together in a Martello tower on the outskirts of Dublin

In the kitchen - "the belly of the house where the family always congregates" - Guy filled me in on the Irish arm of my family. Guy himself had been born in 1947, "that terrible winter when the snow didn't melt till May and they used rashers to light the fire". He spoke of exotic relatives such as Oliver's brother Richard, who moved to Argentina and renamed himself Don Ricardo O'Gogarty. A direct relative of Ricardo named Dermot now ran a prep school in Windsor and was, as far as Guy knew, the only *official* remaining male directly related to Oliver with the surname Gogarty. Information on my great grandmother Mayflo (I was happy to claim her unofficially) was thin. Guy had recently spoken to Noll, Oliver's eldest son, then residing in a nursing home in Dublin. Noll had been reticent about Mayflo declaring only, "She left Ireland in a hurry and died at 103."

Morning stretched to afternoon and Guy's delightful wife, Ann, joined us when she returned from work at Kylemore Abbey. Some Dublin friends drifted in as well as a couple of daughters, a French girl on an exchange visit, another dog and a cat. Before we knew it, we had embarked on one of those Bloomsean odysseys fuelled by prodigious amounts of alcohol that are prosaically known as "sessions" in Ireland.

At around 1am Guy silently rowed us back through a night "As dark a woodland lake-water that mirrors every star" (Oliver St. John Gogarty, "M Love is Dark"). Two swans, also up late, glided by and Guy reminded me of th pair Gogarty, accompanied by W.B.Yeats and President Cosgrave, ceremoniall donated to the Liffey after he had dived into its freezing waters from a high cli to escape an IRA firing squad.

As part of the same campaign, Renvyle, was also razed to the ground i 1923 (and rebuilt). The place, metaphorically, was still on fire when we finall got back to it. A flame-haired boy resembling Mick Hucknell was attacking piano and everyone was singing along whether it was to "The Wild Rover" o Oasis' "Don't Look Back in Anger". Propped on a bar stool, a thousand storie rained down on me. It felt like I'd come home. I staggered upstairs at 2.30am a others were still arriving at the bar. At 4.30 I was woken by loud voices in th corridor and a creaking door. I comforted myself by reminding myself that Yeat and his wife, George, had reputedly laid to rest the Renvyle ghost in a séanc long ago.

In the morning I learned that like all good Irish parties this one had ende around 4am in memorable family squabbles and recriminations.

I half expected swans to again put in an appearance when I visited Ballynakill graveyard which sloped precipitously down to Lough Cartron. When Oliver wa buried, it was noted, a single swan took off, wings beating loudly against th water with the prayers being said. During my visit, light rain was flattening th lake. On a simple tombstone I read.

Oliver St. John Gogarty M.D. 1878-1957
"Our friends go with us as we go
Down the long path where Beauty wends
Where all we love forgathers so
Why should we fear to join our friends?"

CAISTER SOUL WEEKENDER

Land of hope and glory

We finally arrived at the Vauxhall Park Holiday Centre in Norfolk's Caister on-Sea at 8.30pm. From a distance the neat rows of massed caravans looked like cemetery lots until I got a little closer and saw that each of the magnolia and green graves was throbbing to music turned to max. A beefy security man, dressed in black, was directing cars (among them three Porsches, an Aston Martin and a Mercedes). When he introduced himself, I asked him how he got the name "Sparks". "Got blown up by a grenade," he replied matter of-factly.

The Caister Weekender - "the world's longest running and greatest soul music event" - was celebrating its twentieth anniversary but some of those queuing for four days of sweet soul music, getting smashed and maybe copping off hadn't even been born when the first weekender was launched in 1979. Fortunately there were a fair number of vintage models like myself in line too who'd sniffed the scent of new-mown vintage soul. Most of the crowd, judging from the accents, were from Essex. They came in tribes from Romford, Basildon, Southend and Harlow. Carrying their possessions in black plastic bin liners and Adidas bags, they could have been refugees if it weren't for the accompanying boom boxes the size of tanks.

The weekend programme list Sparks handed me outlined the endurance course ahead: thirteen DJs would play classic soul non-stop from 1pm until 4am over the first three days and 1pm-7pm on the Bank Holiday Monday. There would also be a pool party, five-a-side football, the Appalling Talent contest and the epiphanic "Finale" when for two hours the Godfather of British soul, Chris Hill, would conduct the crowd in the Caister version of Last Night at the Proms. The price for the four days including static caravan accommodation was just £90. Finally, at the back of the programme, was a questionnaire with teasers that ranged from "What is the all-time classic soul track?" to "What's the best sex you ever had at Caister, who was it with, and why was it so good?"

Inside the main arena men were dressed with a casual disregard for fashion. A number were rifling through boxes of collectors' records and CDs. Veterans cooed at early 70's Al Green, Howard Melvyn and Jimmy Ruffin sleeves. Those half their age similarly oohed and ahhed at their own generation's classics by the likes of the Brass Construction Company, Lonnie Liston Smith and Maze that had been released a decade later. The dance floor was populated mostly by girls - it was early and most of the boys were in the pool hall or still drinking in their caravans. The token few out on the floor were already dripping, some shirtless, doing their best to keep up.

Slowly, as the new arrivals poured in, Caister built up its head of steam as every new track was greeted with a roar. A number of the revellers, with great dexterity, managed to whoop, dance and balance a drink at the same time.

However, they became noticeably less proficient after the third or fourth double vodka mixed with Red Bull. By midnight it was like dancing in toffee. By 2am fates had been sealed - one couple snogged energetically on a bench next to a boy in a Puma shirt snoring like a drain.

My own soul stripes had been earned in 1967 in Manchester where the *weekender* music event was born (from Friday night at the Twisted Wheel to Stax about 6am on Saturday, then on to Rowntrees in the afternoon and back to the Wheel in the evening). Despite the strong soul tradition in Lancashire, northern voices at Caister were thin on the ground. The most memorable belonged to the Morecambe Hat Posse - Tony the Pup, Larg-in-it Larry, Buster Hymen, Dave the Rave and Sam the Man. The posse wore outlandish hats, had a fondness for water canon wars and drove a battered vintage Escort emblazoned with Soul Injection and Caister Soul Weekender on either wing. Typically for Caister, they were in their mid-thirties and had grown up with the Weekenders.

Tony and Larry both had children but twice a year they headed south "to be kids ourselves again for four days". What drew them, apart from the music - Tony had 1,000 soul albums, 1,000 singles and 300 CDs as well as a definitive library of just about every soul magazine ever produced - was their strong identification with the mixed-race Caister family. While newspapers had recently been filled with racist attacks, Caister was the positive flip-side of modern Britain, a blueprint of racial cohesion and integration rather than polarisation and hatred. Soul music may be primarily made by the American wing of the Black Diaspora, but Caister is a uniquely British phenomenon. The atmosphere in the arena that first night was as mellow as at any British event I've attended. The next morning at around 11am I was woken by someone pushing a wheelie shopping trolley clanking with bottles into the park. Heading in the other direction was a conga of bleary-eyes exiting the camp and dancing through the traffic towards the vast watery outpost of the Norfolk Broads. These were not nature lovers off on a half-day hike, however; they were heading for "hangover fry-ups" at Asda: "£2.79 for ten items - you can't beat that," Buster Hymen said encouraging me to join them, but en route I was sidetracked by a female in pyjamas yelling from the door of a neighbouring caravan, "Oi, come and 'ave a drink."

Roy Ayers was hidden away in some corner singing and there was the unmistakable whiff of recently consumed baked beans on toast. Debbie, Selina - wearing an eye mask - Lisa and Lorna, aged 25-28, were already into their second bottle of vodka. Sitting between them was Martin, another stray invited in who'd requisitioned Lorna's moules. Selina, tipping the rest of the bottle into my glass, told me they'd returned to the caravan around five that morning, continued partying until eight and were now resuming party mode after three hours sleep.

Two of the group were foreign exchange dealers, one was an accountant and the fourth managed a gym in central London. On recent holidays their passports had seen action on a Caribbean cruise and scuba diving in the Red Sea, and there had also been jaunts to New York, Cyprus, Brazil and Barbados. These were Essex girls with the funds to fly anywhere but who wouldn't dream of exchanging *any* holiday for their twice a year Caister jaunts, spending four days cramped in a caravan living on vodka and baked beans.

All of the girls had boyfriends they professed to stay loyal to. "We just come for a girls' weekend," Selina explained. "For the music and the friendship," Debbie chipped in, "We operate an open-door policy like most caravans on the site." The evangelical spirit was spreading like a forest fire; now it was Lisa's turn. "It's the friendliness that's so great here… Not like at clubs where everyone eyeballs you or rucks if someone spills a drink."

On my way to the afternoon swimming pool party, I studied the posters and banners draped across caravans and the pages from magazines blu-tacked to their windows - "Our Father, who art in Canvey, Out loud be heard our name - Seducshun Sexion"; "Hope your Caister is the dog's bollocks - the F'Karwee tribe"; "Willies I have Known", an article ripped from *More!* magazine alongside male pin ups from *Men Unzipped*.

At the poolside, the Morecambe Hatters were blasting Tina's Hen Party from Brentwood (one of four hen parties that Weekender plus a thirty-strong stag party from Charlton). Jean, 35, from caravan 22, continued dancing to Tony Lee's "Reach Up" pounding over the turntable. She'd attended the first Caister Weekender in 1979. "I had a massive Afro and was wild. We used to spray anyone and everyone with shaving foam. Now I'm mellower," she explained while simultaneously pushing Buster Hymen into the water. Jean too was a Caister zealot. "At clubs we've started feeling our age more but here it just gets better every year, reliving the old days, sharing lipstick between the five of us all squeezed round the same mirror."

As I made my way back to the main arena about 10pm on Saturday night I saw the 19 Soul Sisters from Enfield up on one of the chalet balconies having photographs taken. They looked sensational in their purple wigs and black satin outfits, each sporting a single letter from the name of their posse on their backs. One yelled out, "Come and have a drink." Jazz funk was booming out of a bedroom. Lasers were drunkenly careering across the sky.

Saturday is the big party night and many others in the main venue have chosen to dress up. Out on the floor, dancing up a storm are bridal veils, bondage gear, wimples, police uniforms and an inflatable sheep attached to someone's groin. Their owners are black, white, fat, thin, gorgeous and ugly. Each has a family within the Caister family: the AWOL Patrol, the SAS Sisters, Private

Parts, Brixton Front Line, Erection Section, Margate Muff Divers, Funkmaster Generals, Sax Maniacs.

On stage one balding fatty DJ takes over from another: "Sean French, ladies and gentlemen, a big hand but don't let him near your chips." I sit down to take a rest but the seat is moving so violently from the vibration, I have no choice but to head back onto the floor. A nun offers a bride a cigarette and holds the veil up for her with one hand while she lights the cigarette with the other.

Later Chris Hill, the godfather of soul in this country, comes on stage to a roar. "This track and Caister were born here twenty year back." The first bars of "Ain't no stopping us now" are heard and the crowd goes wild. Many have made the twenty-year journey with Chris, some weathering the years better than others but all sharing the same dance floor. Chris spins back-to-back classics and the dance floor heaves. Caister is where people with soul go for their miracles, to have their faith reaffirmed, the communion cup filled with Red Bull and vodka.

If Saturday is the wildest night, Monday's Finale is its epiphany. For two hours Chris, 54 with thinning hair and a face that maps his history, dances like a banshee, miming every instrument and conducting his black and white congregation through flawless renditions of the classics. I remembered what he'd told me earlier in the day. "Black music has come closest in Britain to making us a classless and racially harmonious society." I remembered the Porsches. I remembered Selina and Lisa's holidays, the open-door policy and the queue for Asda breakfasts. "Out on the dancefloor at Caister I see how good it can be - black and white together - and it still gives me a massive buzz."

The cynical may frown, the snobs may snigger at Essex and particularly new-money Essex, but the Caister family are having too good a time to care. The steamy funk and soul plays on. The music may be mostly American but it is a very British affair, a way of living large. The room temperature is 120 degrees. Chris pumps the air and yells, "We are Family." The choir sings every word of every song for two hours. Instead of "Land of Hope and Glory" it's 'Joy and Pain" by Maze, Solo's "Blowing My Mind", Tower of Power's "It Really Doesn't Matter" and the O'Jays "I Love Music". There's hardly a dry eye in the place at the end. After four days of too much music, too much dance, too much laughing, too much junk food, too much drink and not enough sleep, the congregation gathers up its possessions and starts shuffling back out the park for Essex shouting to each other as they go, "See you in October."

DEEP SEA FISHING IN KENYA'S PEMBA CHANNEL

Move over Hemingway and pass the mallet

ur journey forty miles south of Mombasa had been punctuated by shanty markets, a suicidally overloaded ferry and the thrusting hands of beggars. We finally pulled off the main road, following a sign for Lazy Lagoon. It was now ead of night. After ten minutes spin-wheeling along a dirt track we ran out of nd and two arrow-shaped canoes ferried us across water heavy with darkness s we crossed from Kenya to Tanzania. Above us a billion stars were out to guide nd captivate us, scattered round the navigational anchor of the Southern Cross.

Eventually the boats ran ashore at Funzi, ten square miles of tropical island eserved for a few intrepid tourists and 300 locals who eke out a living through absistence fishing and farming.

Barefoot, we followed torchlight, squelching our way through swamp to our ase, the Funzi Island Club, the only guest accommodation on the island but ith room for no more than ten at a time.

The camp consisted of a few concrete, canvas and thatch lodges, located mong cashew trees, mango, tamarind and elephantine baobab. At the centre as an open fire where the only other guests, Mike and Donica, were sitting on gs, sipping Tusker beer and watching bush-babies (small night monkeys) being hased by eight resident Jack Russells.

Donica was a black South Londoner who'd been living with Aussie Mike or three years: "She just turned up one day on the beach and moved in." Mike, ho'd been living in Kenya for twenty years, offered me a beer and then suggested e take me fishing in the creek the next day. Clearly his Aussie roots were still rong: "No 'birds' allowed though ... fishing is strictly blokes only."

I accepted his offer and did not mention my only other fishing expedition, ged seven to a pond in Shropshire. My father had painstakingly shown me how bait a hook and cast a line but when, after several eternities, I found a fish angling at the end of my rod, I simply threw it into the water and fled. My rother, to coin an expression, was a different kettle of fish, and endlessly broke cords for pike. Patrick was in the Hemingway mould. I was more in the Beatrix otter mould. Mike was like my brother but more brash and macho - tanned, lver shoulder length hair, stocky frame... you know the kind of thing: a cross etween heroic Norseman and Aussie misogynist.

The following afternoon when Mike, dressed only in a wrap-round kikoy n African sarong), stood up in our dugout to cast his line, the two women in ur party (he had relented on the boys-only rule) swooned. Donica meanwhile t gorgeously at the prow trailing her line nonchalantly through the mangrove-ained water while we newcomers tried to make sense of the cabalistic science of atchets, brakes, spindles, lures, weights and lines.

Mike had spent half his life earning a Kenyan living by tour guiding, fishing d making furniture. Now that the safari hunters had all turned conservationists

and were busily telling the locals they mustn't hunt, the sea was where tho
riding Hemingway's wake now span out their African fantasies. Pre-eminent
the pescatory dreamscape was the marlin, which, Mike reluctantly admitted, I
still hadn't managed to land - "Caught a 72lb sailfish and speared a 50lb group
though."

It was highly unlikely that we were going to match either feat pootling
a channel in a canoe even if Mike claimed that 20lb Jacks and barracuda we
lurking beneath us.

As I expected, we didn't get a nibble. Mike knew the reason. "Told you y
shouldn't have let the birds come. Sheilas always bring bad luck."

Personally I was rather relieved although I didn't admit this to Mike. I w
more than happy chatting, watching the egrets, fish eagles, assorted kingfishe
and Donica while the sun plummeted behind the mangrove.

Mike, who claimed that in his days as a safari tour guide he had been know
as Captain Africa, had crossed the Sahara seven times, worked with gorillas
Rwanda and ridden on the back of a thirty-foot basking shark. He therefo
advised me to be a little more adventurous: "Go on a proper deep sea fishing tr
out in the Pemba Channel; it's got the best fishing along the entire seaboard."

After a couple of indolent days lazing on the blaze of white beach, lazin
on a house boat in the Funzi Channel, lazily viewing baby crocs from a can
on the Ramisis river and lazily lazing around camp, I decided to take up Mik
suggestion and booked a deep sea fishing trip. Mike unfortunately could n
accompany me ("Got to go to a bloody wedding").

I reached the 44-foot twin diesel White Otter, anchored offshore, at 6.30a
Saidi, the skipper, had worked on board for 27 years, Kadi had been at the hel
for thirty years and Abi, preparing the barracuda bait for the lighter lines, w
the rooky with just eight months service under his belt. The White Otter its
was 35 years old and had reputedly landed over 1100 Marlin: more than an
other fishing boat on the East African coast.

As we headed out into the open sea, white water fanning behind chased I
the early morning sun, I studied the logbook. An 800lb black marlin and 724
blue marlin had been landed as well as Kenya's record tiger shark (984 lbs). Th
Pemba Channel where we were heading was a natural corridor between Pemb
Island (Tanzania) and the mainland (Kenya) that was apparently teeming wi
billfish. So how come, I pondered, in 176 days fishing last season, the Whi
Otter had only landed 32 marlin (and 61 sailfish) according to the log? That w
one marlin for every six trips and with up to five fishermen per trip, I calculat
my odds of landing a marlin at 30:1. It wasn't encouraging.

The coastline became a smeared pencil line and then disappeared. At th
stern five rods thrust heavenwards like prayer flags, fitted with Everoll reels a

0, 50 and 30lb lines. They formed a semicircle around the "fighting chair" which, bolted to the floor, complete with harness and vicious looking truncheon, reminded me of an electric chair on death row

As we sped away from the ever rising sun, Saidi ran through when, if and how to strike once a fish took the lure. He then proceeded to spin stories. Saidi was skippering the boat when the 800lb black marlin first bit eight years ago. It had then taken seven hours to land the monster as it got trapped in the line. His story brought back memories of Moby Dick when the great white whale rose pinioned in the turns upon turns in which, during the past night, the whale had reeled the involutions of the lines around him".

Suddenly, as if on cue, there was a shout from above. A fish arched through the air, one of the 50lb lines started running and, before I knew what I was doing, I found myself first to the rod.

"Let it run, let it run," I heard Saidi shout. "Release the brake a little."

The main dangers were that the fish, whatever it was, would shed the hook or that the line would break. At last the line stopped running and I began gingerly to lift and lower the rod, reeling in as fast as I could.

The butt of the rod dug painfully into my stomach and my back was praying the thing would escape. I sensed a great deal of commotion behind me and soon a temporary harness was being waved in front of me. I slipped one arm in and then the other. The harness was quickly fastened and I was able to slot the rod into a metal gimbal that resembled a large thimble, at the front of the belt. Said motioned me to the fighting chair where I transferred the rod into a fixed gimbal, shaped like an outsized codpiece, and with an angled foot rest to push against I was now able to settle in for the struggle.

For more than an hour the fish tried to escape its fate, barrelling down through the half-mile deep channel where it then tried to rest, only to find it was being reeled back inexorably towards the surface. Once it realised the proximity of its adversary, it leaped out of the water - its back arching, its bill pointing skyward - before crashing through the water and plummeting once more to the depths.

Sweat poured off me, the sun beat down, my arms screamed with the effort, but I was now engaged in a primeval struggle and something deep inside me insisted it was a battle I could not lose.

Eventually I managed to reel the fish in close to the boat where, like a bolt of lightning, Saidi speared its shank with the gaff and heaved it aboard with the help of other crew members.

Once on board its skull was summarily cracked open like an egg with the wooden mallet. Its mouth sucked desperately at the air. Its eyes stared accusingly. As Said started wrapping it in a tarpaulin shroud, I recalled how I first saw it taking the lure, its body electric blue from the adrenaline rushing through it. felt awful. I had landed a 152lb black marlin, but after the excitement of th chase and the beauty of the fish seemingly walking across the water on its tail now there was just brutality and death.

Saidi had dismissed the option of tagging the fish and letting it go; it ha been badly torn and was exhausted - an obvious target for sharks. "You only release a fish with a chance of survival," he explained. I donated the fish to th crew who sold it to the fishing co-operative and it ended up on plates at the loca village.

We headed back to the White Otter's base at the Pemba Channel Fishin Club where we lunched among the fishing trophies, chalkboard records and mounted heads. After lunch a picture was taken of me standing dwarfed by th suspended ten-foot marlin next to a chalkboard which recorded the details o my catch. Peter Ruysenaars, owner of the Club, explained that the skill of dee sea fishing lay in catching as big a fish as possible with the lightest possible line He clearly didn't want me getting above my station, "The record is a 724lb blu marlin caught on a 50lb line like yours."

The next morning, with a blister on my finger and aching arms, I visite Mike and Donica at their Tiwi beachfront home. When Mike heard my news, hi eyes rolled. "I don't believe it. I just don't believe it." His gills turned transparen green. "Twenty years I've been after one and you, a Pom, come out not knowing one end of a rod from the other and land a bloody marlin."

D PRYNN'S STONEHENGE

The angels' landing strip

Ed Prynn lives in a bungalow a mile outside St Merryn in Cornwall. The only difference between Ed and his neighbours is that he happens to have Stonehenge sitting in his garden and likes to dress in the white robe of a Druid priest.

Over the past four decades Ed has squeezed onto his front lawn a number of monoliths he proudly calls his rock sculptures. Taking pride of place is an 18 ton dolmen he calls The Angels' Runway. One night, according to Ed, he was woken by an angel who sat on his bed complaining of night time navigational difficulties and bemoaning the lack of safe landing places in the area. Ed, always eager to help, constructed his dolmen as a landing strip. "The angels run up the capstone like them Harrier jets on aircraft carriers and jump off," he explains. "Soon I'm going to rig up some fairy lights so they can see it better after dark."

Ed's "rock sculptures" have transformed a nondescript suburban garden into an occult fantasy sufficiently intriguing to passers-by that he now supplements his disability pension (Ed is partially sighted) with donations from visitors. The contributions may not amount to much but then Ed's needs are modest apart from the occasional boulder he might require shipping from the Preseli Mountains or somewhere further afield.

The most exotic stones are a pair of émigrés from the Falklands. During the war with Argentina, Ed wrote to Governor Sir Rex Hunt asking if he might spare a rock or two for a memorial he wanted to erect to the war dead. St Merryn's cynics laughed on hearing about the letter but were silenced when two quartz rocks weighing a ton each arrived having been transported 8000 miles on the MS *Lesterbrook*.

Ed believes his Falkland Memorial has special powers. But then he believes all his stones have. Each of the seven that make up the Stone Circle are named after powerful women in his life and it is from these women, Ed claims, that the rocks get their energy. "Great Auntie Hilda, named after the seventh of my mother's father's sisters, is strongest of all - the seventh sister is always lucky," Ed explains.

According to Ed, the most popular "sculpture" with visitors is the Rocking Stone. "People stand rocking on it for hours for good luck." To underline the point, Ed jumps on board, his white druid's robe swaying round his ankles, his shock of white hair iridescent in the sun. "It weighs more than ten ton and rocks like a feather in the wind. Now tell me that's not magic."

Another monolith, an Italian marble slab called the Judgement Stone apparently received its power from the sea having been washed by it daily for over a hundred years before being dragged by tractor from a nearby cove to his home. Ed believes it has enormous power. "In some future time all the world leaders are going to be drawn by it to my home to heal the world's sickness."

One political figure has already called in. Unfortunately Ed didn't know who Dennis Healey was when he paid an impromptu visit ("'Who be you?' I asked him - embarrassing it were"). Others have been invited: Prince Charles' brief, polite apology is pinned to the garage wall and alongside it is an even briefer note from Margaret Thatcher - "I called but no one was there." Ed had invited the former prime minister when she was holidaying in nearby Constantine Bay. "Unfortunately my mother made me go and do the shopping and I missed her," Ed shakes his head still crestfallen.

Sharing the garage wall with these apologies are plaques dedicated to benefactors and to an assortment of celebrities that Ed and girlfriend Glynnis believe have made "a positive contribution to life on earth". The Hall of Fame quickly outgrew the garage and now slate plaques cover every inch of the bungalow's facade. It is an eclectic collection: Harry Houdini, Benny Hill (Ed's voice sounds uncannily like Benny Hill in "The Fastest Milkman in the West"), Frank Ifield, Sir William Hesketh Lever ("I like Sunlight soap") and a Billy Butlin redcoat named Jonathan Cowling.

Ed encourages me to climb through the Marriage Stone. "Shame your wife's not here. It's a fertility stone and many ladies climb through it with tremendous results." I tell him that our two teenage children are enough for us. "Well if you ever decide to re-marry, I do marriage contracts too. My tip to newlyweds is to not go too heavy to start: just get married for a week; if it's going good, have another week, and then a month."

The marriages take place in a grotto Ed has dug ten feet underground, which he sagely informs me is the womb of mother earth, as we descend the stone steps. "We do rebirthing here too." At the central circular chamber is a lingam fertility stone. "We call it 'The Dreckly Stone 'cos it guarantees you better luck *dreckly*... I came up on Ernie premium bonds not so long back after a visit. It were only £50 but we tore our clothes off and thanked the stone."

As we enter Ed's bedroom, a black Collie called Roly runs out. At the centre of the room is a pine four-poster bed which appears too large for the room. Above it is hung a purple Lurex canopy decorated with sequins in the shape of a well-endowed fertility god in a clear state of excitement. "I did that," Ed's partner Glynnis proudly informs me. "It's a celestial bed - makes you sexier." She smiles and lifts a candlewick bedspread that conceals a mammoth crystal sleeping beneath the mattress. "That's where the power comes from." Draped across the mummified crystal is the lead of an electric blanket that serves as the back-up if the crystal fails to warm love makers up.

Following our tour of the bungalow ("the most photographed in Cornwall", according to Ed, "and possibly in the whole of the UK"), Glynnis leads me across the garden with a twitching hazel stick. She's trying to locate their underground spring. "Every time I stray into the Stone Circle the stick has a fit." She demonstrates and the stick does indeed become possessed. "See, see - that's the power of them stones," Ed excitedly exclaims before insisting on dancing with me inside the stone circle. "Keep your eyes on the tops of the stones, Paul. D'you feel it, d'you feel it?"

Ed now has plans for a new sculpture: "It's going to be a big log and I'm going to call it Big Dick. He's also planning a tea room which he'll call The Happy Fanny after his Great Great Granny Fanny.

As I leave Ed and Glynnis' bungalow an hour later, Ed waves me off: "There you're a druid now so make sure you come back for the next sun dance on the summer solstice - it'll be great fun but watch you don't get no mystic mania. Some people can go over the top a bit."

FRESH OM

Hampi New Year

66I could feel the soft vibration a mile before arriving in Hampi. It was oceanic … it was like … it was like my body was making love to the sea."

It could have been Goa, circa the hippy-dippy 1960s. In fact, it was the fag end of the millennium and I was in Karnataka, 225 dusty miles and a nine-hour drive inland from Baga Beach and Anjuna. I was standing inside the courtyard of the Shanti guesthouse, one of a string of budget travellers' lodges that stand on the site of old Vijayanagar, once the heart of the mightiest and largest Hindu empire on the Indian subcontinent.

The Swiss woman was sitting on the floor outside her cell-like room; her polka-dot loons folded beneath her, her Star of David t-shirt more faded than the wall she was leaning against. Above her was a hand-painted sign warning guests about narcotics, advising them to lock their doors and discouraging them from walking around town alone with valuables.

Sasha had returned to staring at a small black plastic digital travel clock. I wondered if she was meditating on time. "Can't get the bloody thing to work," she answered my quizzical stare and I immediately thought of Harry Lime's neat summation of Switzerland's obsession and legacy: "In Italy for thirty years under the Borgias they had warfare, terror, murder, bloodshed - they produced Michelangelo, Leonardo da Vinci and the Renaissance. In Switzerland they had brotherly love, 500 years of democracy and peace, and what did they produce? The cuckoo clock."

Eight weeks earlier Sasha had given up her job and apartment in Zurich to find herself in India but clearly still hadn't quite managed to slough the Swiss obsession with punctiliousness.

Sasha had headed hotfoot to Hampi. "I planned spending just a few days but soon it was a week and another week… My body keeps telling me to stay longer. The place hums. My body feels like a cello playing celestial music." She paused meaningfully. "The other day I visited another town and the music stopped." With oceanic sex and celestial music on tap, I could understand Sasha's reluctance to move on.

Hampi's humming made me think back to the carefully crayoned diagrams of cosmic vibrations Sadashiva Yogi, Hampi's most eminent guru, had shown me earlier that day at the Shivananda Yogashram Homoeo & Magneto Therapy Centre. Having offered me a pollution-removing magneto session in what looked like an executioner's chair complete with metal wrist shackles, the yogi, aged 61, opened the book he was currently writing on the psychology of yoga.

"The world is a point of dust and a magnet and so are we." He rocked his knees gently as if in time to some internal mantra and stared out from the balcony to the ghats of the Tungabhadra river below. "…The stone thrown outside the world's gravity doesn't fall." He paused and stopped rocking. "Through correct breathing we too can change our way of being and stop falling. By breathing correctly our third eye will open like a flower and remain open." The connection between the physics of the universe, our breathing, an additional eye and psychic tumbling were a little too advanced for me. Like Sasha I needed more time in Hampi.

The yogi was a big fan of the Vijayanagara Empire. "There was great learning then - you can still feel the knowledge in every temple and stone. Knock and it will open." He returned to looking out over the river. I offered a donation to the ashram which he politely refused. "I already have everything." Instead, he gave me four bananas, one of which I chomped on meditatively sitting on the steps of the ghats waiting for the door to open.

Whilst North Goa has become a numinous Ibiza, Hampi remains the genuine article, a clearing house of fakers and fakirs, gurus and spiritual pilgrims from the east and west and all corners between. For a brief moment in the 1990s, it looked like it would follow North Goa into techno eclipse as it was buried beneath the drug haze of full-moon and New Year parties organised by Israelis who'd slipped the straightjacket of military service back home. But in 1995 there was a police clampdown and New Year celebrations were now as demure as those in Kent.

Today was December 31 and I had been assured by savvy travellers that the Vijayanagar guesthouse across the river would be the only party worth going to.

There was still plenty of time, though, so I descended to Hampi Bazaar, a half-mile long strip lined with cheap restaurants and Kashmiri handicraft shops. One seller offered me a 600-year-old Parvati bronze for £9 - it had probably been cast in the back room that morning. At the cafés, travellers in draw-string cotton trousers and vests sat on stools choking on bidis whilst Indian visitors smoked their Marlboros. I ordered a Coke at the Shree Venkateshwara Restaurant and asked two girls covered in henna tattoos if they knew of anything happening that evening.

Stella ("The star not the girl's name"), from Bromsgrove, wrinkled her nose stud. "Squat. Squat's on. That's what's on." Her friend looked up from scribbling designs in a notebook. "I'm a fabric designer," she explained. A more permanent dolphin tattoo swam about on her shoulder. She wore a leather ankle bracelet and had cropped ginger hair. A female Indian guide resting with two middle-aged Israeli guests at the next table interrupted to tell me that my long toe nails (I was wearing sandals) indicated that I was alert and courageous. The girls looked momentarily confused and then returned to the subject in hand. "We're still looking for something ourselves tonight." Claude, taking up the third corner of the table, replete with French beard, locks and hippy mirror bag, lowered his voice and leaned towards me. "Don't tell anyone but the Gobi is doing something special." He raised an eyebrow meaningfully. "Boring," Brummy cast her verdict.

The Chinese whisper culture - "don't tell anyone but…" - is as endemic to travellers' folklore as amoebic dysentery. The third disease that flourishes on the subcontinent is constantly worrying about what you're missing and thinking you should be somewhere else. Brummy continued to worry. "Should have stayed in Anjuna, they've got a four-day tribal party that's starting right now." I thought of the American poet John Berryman's "Dream Song 251": "Once a fellow dinner guest and I reckoned up merely what each missed during his months in India: together we made the whole subcontinent sigh."

I decided to stick with my original plan of heading out to the Vijayanagar guesthouse. As I walked back along Hampi Bazaar, a conga of black-shirted pilgrims were just entering the Virupaksha temple which had been garlanded in harsh bare bulbs. The living temple was resounding to trance-like music that had nothing to do with Anjuna - a three-foot drum pounded, a ten-foot brass bell rang and somewhere a trumpet played a tune that would get the most obstinate of cobras dancing. The Mussolini Black Shirts were chanting as they entered the temple.

It was now 8pm and a circular coracle was ferrying people across the river to see in the New Year. Five years ago there was nothing on the far bank, now every month a new lodge seems to open. Five of us sailed beneath a fat moon, sharing a floating basket not dissimilar to the one the baby Moses travelled in.

Three of my fellow sailors were Londoners who had just arrived in town. One, a second generation Indian beauty from Southall, dressed in western hippy gear, adopted a slow precise pidgin to ask the boatman, "Do you know where Babu's is?" The friends were looking for a guesthouse. The boatman mistakenly thought she was referring to a temple. "Nooooo… with b-e-d-s," she tried to clarify things. The last word unmoored into separate syllables and bobbed across the water unanswered.

As we pulled into the bank I noticed a shaven headed, gaunt westerner in dhoti performing puja at the water's edge beside two attendant buffalo. I peeled off the track into the garden of the Vijayanagar guesthouse where westerners were reverentially looking out over the river as they munched and drank. Behind them, oblivious to the view and sprawled on a tarpaulin, were around fifty local Hampi men dressed in white dhotis and white shirts drinking, chatting loudly, playing cards and enjoying their own New Year's Eve party.

Jean-Michel Jarre crap was playing. The beers flowed and I flowed between the two camps. Inevitably it was the Indians who invited me to sit and join and share their drinks. In the western camp I recognised Will and Stuart, home-counties boys I'd met the day before. They invited me to pull up a chair and introduced me to Sal, Martin, Ian and Marie-Claire who were talking about Pondicherry as they passed round a spliff. "Yeah, Pondicherry would be cool,"

Martin nodded his head. Marie-Claire, with a dancing French accent, pitched in. "I wish I was in Anjuna. They're having a four-day party." I heard the subcontinent sigh again. Sal, however, was enjoying being where she was. "I'm kinda glad there's no techno party. It would be out of place."

I sailed back on my petal across the river at 2am. Outside the Moonlight Restaurant, a girl aged around eight was writing with coloured sand: "Wish You Happy New Year".

GARCIA LORCA'S ALGIERS

The outsider

Yes, I was surprised too to learn that Federico García Lorca grew up in Algiers. Hard to imagine how an Andalucian poet, cut down in his prime by one of Franco's firing squads, had managed to squeeze in an Algerian childhood. Still, I'd already been reliably informed that Jean-Paul Belmondo and François Mitterand's mum had also spent their childhoods in Algiers. Oh, and Yves Saint Laurent, according to my companions Mohammed and Ben Mohammed. But it was Albert Camus, the only Algerian I'd ever heard of, and my existential hero from my late-pimples years, whom I had come to track down.

On my Air Algiers flight out, I finished re-reading the diary of Isabelle Eberhardt, *The Passionate Nomad*. If a nineteenth-century Russian-Swiss anorexic would adopt Algeria, Islam and male clothing to indulge a penchant for the desert and kief (marijuana and pleasure are the same word in Arabic), then what held Camus enthralled so long had to be pretty special. That was the quest I'd pitched to the travel editor - discovering Albert Camus' Algiers.

In reality I already knew the country well. Tracking Camus may have been my ostensible angle but I had another, more sentimental, reason for my visit. Twenty years earlier, as a newly qualified teacher, I took up my first job teaching English at the lycée in Draa El Mizan in the foothills of the Djudjura Mountains in Algeria's Grande Kabylie region.

During the year I spent there, I became friends with my fellow nomadic teachers drawn from France, Belgium and the Middle East, but in the early summer things turned nasty. The boarders at the school, which catered for a large catchment area, went on strike because senior school officials were diverting funds, resulting in the kids enduring prison-like conditions and gruel while the proviseur and headmaster swanned around in fancy new Peugeots.

The majority of the expat teachers showed solidarity by joining the students in the playground. However, strikes were forbidden in Algeria and so the senior management knew all they needed was a scapegoat to blame, and they could return to illegally augmenting their salaries.

Within 24 hours the foreign teachers, along with the head boy, were identified as the ringleaders and counter revolutionaries. Mohammed disappeared. A month later he returned with burn marks at his temples. He had been incarcerated in the mental hospital, Dar El Beida. The name translates as the white house, and I imagine white light was all Mohammed was seeing after his electric shock treatment. The only words he could utter, repeatedly, were "Il me semble… il me semble…" ("It seems to me… it seems to me…"). As far as I know, he never learned to say anything else.

The overseas teachers meanwhile had letters opened, phone calls tapped and we had to contact our embassies daily to inform them we were still safe and had not been arrested. Eventually one teacher, a Belgian, disappeared. It was a paranoid and dangerous time and I quit the country secretly by ferry from Oran in July vowing to never return.

But the huge beauty of the country remained a stronger memory than that brief nightmare and now I was back again. Algeria is as vast as it is dramatic and there was still bits I hadn't seen. Top of my list was Tassili n'Ajjer which, though still in Algeria, is as far from Algiers as London is.

Nowadays in the Sahara, the Tuaregs have traded their camels for Toyota Land Cruisers and it was in one of these, returning from a trek in the Tassili n'Ajjer, the world's largest outdoor art gallery with 15,000 prehistoric paintings spread across a national park larger than Switzerland, that a fellow local journalist asked me what had drawn me to Algeria.

"I just wanted to see the Tassili."

"Is that what you're writing about?"

"No, I'm here to do a piece tracing Camus' life in Algiers."

Ben Mohammed, who worked for the largest Algerian daily, *El Moudjahid*, and had somehow inveigled his way into our jeep, motioned a finger down his throat and simulated chucking up. I believe Ben Mohammed's "Bwqerrrrk" to have been Berber even though I know he spoke not a word of it. Finally regaining control of his vocal cords, he spat out, "Albert Camus' Algiers? Algiers was never Albert Camus'." And then as an afterthought he added, "What did *he* write anyway?" I reeled off *The Outsider*, *The Rebel*, *The Fall*, *The Plague*. Ben Mohammed was unmoved. "But what did he *really* write?!" His left eyebrow shot up in a sneering exclamation mark over the last word, inviting no further discussion. "Anyway the man wasn't a good man."

I met up with Ben Mohammed and his friend Mohammed again in a café in Algiers a couple of days later when he expounded further on Camus' worthlessness. Algeria's only Nobel Prize winner (and, unlikely legend has it, once goalkeeper for the national football team) had fallen irrevocably from grace when, constantly pressed by the National Liberation Front to come out unequivocally behind them and disown his *pied noir* French colonist origins, he finally admitted after a spate of FLN bombings of Europeans, "I'm against this revolution because if I have to choose between justice and my mother I choose my mother." He fell like a brick, despite being the only journalist who had earlier reported the French atrocities.

Ben Mohammed led me backstage into the National Theatre where two actors told me, "No, we have never performed anything by Albert Camus. Nor on Camus. Brecht yes, Shakespeare yes, Camus no." "But Brecht and Shakespeare weren't Algerian," I pointed out. "No ...was Camus?" one asked in amazement.

Next I popped into the British Council and chatted to a couple of teaching recruits. They talked about wind surfing up the coast at Tamentfoust and male

arassment in the street but neither had heard of Camus. "Maybe he lives on the
ther side of town."

That afternoon Mohammed and I walked past tailgating traffic whose wing
mirrors were all snapped shut like clams. At the old Rue de Lyon in the Belcourt
istrict we found no record of Camus' impoverished existence. The road signs
ere all in Arabic and the Rue de Lyon had long since been bequeathed to some
martyr of the revolution. There was no plaque at number 93. No footprint in the
and. Meursault, no doubt, would have approved.

I tracked down a bookshop that was supposedly run by an old French woman
ho knew Camus. Its shutters were padlocked and its owner had either moved
n to heaven or another part of town. It was at this point in our investigations
hat Mohammed, never the most forbearing of companions, suggested I switch
o Lorca. "Lorca?" I asked, incredulous. "Yes, he studied at my old lycée on the
utskirts of town."

I temporarily bade farewell to my companion who had a film to watch on
able TV that his apartment block "liberated from Bordeaux" via an illegal Swiss
eceiver. We arranged to meet later and I took off to browse three substantial
ookshops on Didouche Mourad. Hoping to find Lorca's Algerian memoirs
nd certain to uncover numerous biographies on Camus, I discovered only *The
Complete Works of Thomas Hardy*, *Psychiatric Rating Scales* and *Ten Pin Bowling*
third edition) in English. By way of consolation, I bought myself a comic in
rench whose celebration of the heroes of "The Battle of Algiers" reminded me
f my own childhood "Arnie Knott Takes Arnhem".

My pursuit of ghosts came to an end on a hill of millionaires and embassies.
n a sound-proofed office, Dr Youssef Nacib, Director General of University
ublications and Albert Camus expert, confirmed, "I'm afraid that for Camus,
lgiers was everything but for Algiers, Camus is nothing." Dr Nacib had read
Camus' dissertation for his philosophy diploma. "You could tell the man was a
enius then. We are poorer for his loss but you must remember the liberation
truggle only ended in 1962. Wounds have not yet healed." I decided to switch
o Lorca but Dr Nacib was as surprised as I had been to learn that the Andalucian
oet was in fact Algerian. Together we looked up a literary who's who to find he
ad never even been to Algeria. Mohammed, who had been waiting outside for
e, was unabashed. "It must have been another García Lorca."

HENLEY-ON-TODD REGATTA, ALICE SPRINGS

You Poms don't know how to throw a proper paddle

Seventy per cent of Australia is arid and Alice Springs lies pretty much at the centre of the parched dustbowl, a misanthropic concrete outpost over 900 miles from any body of water worth dipping your toes in. Known as the Red Heart of the country, to the Aussie way of thinking it was thus the obvious choice when it came to hosting the nation's annual regatta.

On our three-hour flight from Sydney, my nephew Tony described what I could expect. "Unlike the Henley Pom version, our river is dry so locals do their best to make up for this by knocking back oceans of alcohol. When they're drunk enough, they pick up boats they've built out of beer cans, pull 'em up round their waists like rubber rings and then race each other - usually falling over a fair bit - across the dry riverbed."

Tony ran through the race programme: rowing eights, fours, Oxford tubs, yachts and bath tubs. "It's pretty eclectic," he added. "The Australia Cup is probably the most prestigious. Rules are strict but kept to a minimum or no one would remember - you gotta run inside the boat and finish with the same number of crew you started with. That's about it. After the races they have a big naval fight with flour and water cannon." Tony drew breath before summing up, "It's basically a piss-up in a bottomless boat. Makes you proud to be Australian." Tony, who hailed from Preston but had been working in Sydney for close on a decade, had clearly gone native.

We were dressed in shorts and t-shirts expecting temperatures of around 35°C, dust and persistent flies. When we arrived, it was raining - the first rain Alice had seen in four months. On the flight I'd read that the one and only time the event was cancelled was in 1993 because the Todd river had flooded after a heavy rainstorm. "A bottomless boat just doesn't work on water. But no worries," Tony reassured me, "this is just a cloudburst and will be over in half a tick."

For our first evening in town we'd pre-booked an "under-the-stars concert with bush tucker". Unfortunately it was cancelled because of the rain. We tried to switch to a camel trek out into the bush for a damp barbie but found that was cancelled too. Apparently camels - those ships of the desert - don't care for rain. I would have thought they'd love it.

We borrowed a couple of oilskins and an umbrella from our hotel and splodged along a muddy riverbed dotted with ghost gums. On one trunk someone had tacked a notice: "No Diving". A few homeless drunk Aborigines lumbered in their inimitable post-apocalyptic haze. The rain by now had moved up a notch from drizzle to serious. Eventually we spotted a boat, a cross between a Mississippi paddleboat and a gunboat, which was due to see action in the grand finale "Battle of the Boats" the following day when a 4-wheel drive chassis would sneak it up on enemies and blast them with flour mortars and high-pressure water cannon.

Nearby, a posse of rather disconsolate individuals shuffled feet, staring up into the heavens. I asked one of the group what was happening. "We're deliberating," he said enigmatically and returned to his cloud gazing. I wandered off to join Tony who had tracked down the coordinator of the event, Bill van Dijk, a Dutch émigré with equally prodigious paunch and beard. The Commodore informed us it was raining even harder up at the head of the river and the chances of the regatta going ahead were slim. "It'll probably flood," he summed up. I couldn't believe it.

What do you do when you've travelled half way round the world for an event and it gets cancelled? Plan B - the under-the-stars concert - had already been cancelled too, and Plan C - the camel trek - had similarly bitten the mud. We set our compasses for the course most Alice citizens seem to take daily, even without such provocation, and headed off to get drunk.

A number of the party in the riverbed were heading up to the Federal Sports Club. We tagged along. Propping up the bar were identikit blokes in broad-brimmed hats, knee-length socks and Stubbies (obscenely tight, green, ziples shorts). A mere handful of women were present, dressed in floral-patterned frocks. As rain played its tympani on the tin roof, I struck up conversation with Reg Smith. "Shame about the Regatta," I opened. "Saves going out in the rain anyway," Reg phlegmatically replied. "Yesterday it was 35 degrees." That made me feel a lot better.

I ordered a round of drinks - dinky "butchers" for Reg ("I like smaller glasses so the beer keeps cooler; I just order a lot of 'em - gotta keep your fluids up"), "a handle" (a 10oz beer with a handle) for another couple sharing our table, and pints (rather grandly referred to as "reputed pints" and measuring only two thirds our imperial pint) for Tony and myself who were in a hurry to catch up.

Reg, 71 years old and now retired, wore the regulation knee-length white socks and Stubbies, together with an impressive beard and a liver-spotted bald pate. After being demobbed in '46, I discovered, he became a meteorologist out at the airstrip where he also lived. "We had three sealed runways and only two flights coming in a week," he drawled in an accent as flat and featureless as the desert he inhabited. "There wasn't a whole lot to do so we dreamed up land yachting using boards and bike wheels to pass our time and make more use of the airstrip. In 1962 we turned it into the first Henley-on-Todd for the Rotary."

I was aghast. By sheer chance I'd stumbled on the man who'd invented the Regatta. To celebrate I ordered another round of drinks.

In early racing days, Reg would ensure he had the outside track so he could force those on the inside closer to the gum trees where they "got their heads whacked off by the branches". He smiled nostalgically. "We won a fair few races before they made the course straight and the fitter, younger kids started winning.

By the time Tony and I left the Federal Sports Club, golf balls were hammering on the roof. We moved on to a pub, the Todd Tavern, which Bruce Chatwin in *Songlines* had claimed was the most memorable in town. The bar was jumping. Men in kangaroo hats, each with a more monstrous girth than the last, shot pool and abused each other foully and cheerfully. At the bar I squeezed between two bodies. A head swung round as if only connected to its shoulders by a thread. Its owner's eyes were unmoored and blinking as if trying to bring me into range. The beast was wearing a threadbare colourless t-shirt on which a garland of flies spelled out Alice Springs. Beside his stuttering elbow, on the bar, lay a beer-stained journalist's notebook and pen. "What d'you want?" he slurred. I told him a beer and then realised he was not offering a drink. Being a reasonable bar survivor, I quickly offered instead to buy him one and we immediately became best friends.

Michael worked at the local newspaper, the *Centralian Advocate*, hated Alice, hated Jeff Kennett (the Victorian Premier who hailed from the state), hated the Rotary Club which organises the Regatta, hated Elton John and most of all hated Poms. He was also very drunk. Michael was an outcast even in this town of outcasts so he was not going to miss out on company. He started organising our night for us. Tony told him we'd already booked to eat at the Overlanders and he informed us the owner was "a complete and utter bastard". He staggered with us down the street, through Alice's solitary shopping mall, to Scotty's, a smaller, darker dive in Todd Mall whose walls were festooned with black and white photographs of local settlers. Michael was starting to come apart at the seams and we excused ourselves after two more drinks and left him to explode, promising to visit his office the next morning at the *Advocate* for unlikely "croissant and coffee".

Overlanders, was a robust, outbackery kind-of-place with timber beams, paddle fans, cattle pelts splayed on the walls and Jackaroos and Jillaroos singing drovers' songs such as "Home among the Gum Trees". Everybody was hurtling beautifully into Friday night oblivion. Tony ordered us a platter of camel fillet, crocodile vols-au-vent, kangaroo fillet and emu medallion. Several more beers and wines down the line, four rather loud women on the next table invited themselves over to ours. One of the party, a rather plump lady, leant over Tony and spilled her bits into his lap giggling, "Hey mate, you can climb up my drainpipe anytime you like." Tony finished the bottle of wine he was drinking from the neck and in some haste excused us. "Gotta meet a mate." "Oh yeah?" the well-endowed lady challenged. "Who?" "Some journalist called Michael." "That little shit! What d'you wanna hang out with that psycho for? You gay or sommit?"

As we walked home through the teeming rain, Bruce Chatwin's understated description of Alice Springs came to mind: "Alice is not a very cheerful town either by day or night." The Alice, as it's usually known, started out life in 1870 as a staging post for the overland telegraph line. Telegraph poles seemed about all it was good for.

I woke a few times during the night, and each time drifted back to sleep to the sound of rain hammering on the metal roof. In the morning it was still at it. Down at reception, we learned the inevitable - the Regatta had been cancelled. Gloom descended.

With nothing better to do, we visited Michael's newspaper office. He wasn't there. Probably in bed nursing some hangover the size of the Northern Territories. We breakfasted nearby in Swingers where the wall was covered in pictures of breasts decorated with pins, zips, rings and tattoos. We thought it a normal kind of red-blooded Oz male greasy spoon. It was in fact a lesbian café serving fresh juices and wholesome muesli. Next we decided to visit the Old Gaol (now museum), as I'd read a quote by Bertrand Russell which stated that everyone in town ended up there at some time or other during their stay. The noticeboard declared it open; two heavyweight padlocks argued more persuasively otherwise.

We slogged up Anzac Hill in the drizzle and looked out over the dank five-street grid of aluminium warehouses, multi-storey car park, American shopping mall and cadaverous-looking ghost gums. In the distance stood the crumpled ridges of the MacDonnell Ranges. On a noticeboard at the top of the war memorial we read, "If you see the Todd flow three times, you will not leave Alice." In the river bed, trickles were joining up with sinister intent, sweeping up jettisoned wine boxes and beer bottles.

Slowly things improved - not the weather, but the day. We visited the Pioneer Women's Hall of Fame where, amongst photographs of petticoated cameleers, fearsome early female dentists and bull rodeo riders, we drooled over a publicity shot of Lottie Lyell, star of the 1919 Australian classic, *The Sentimental Bloke*.

Next we headed out of town, to visit the Frontier Camel Farm where the camels were on strike. "Forty-five degrees and they're happy as Larry, one drop of rain and you try getting 'em to budge," owner Nick Smail, in bush hat and Ned Kelly oilskin, complained as he selected a new strip of smoked camel from his Jerky packet to chew. Nick and wife Michelle make the Jerky themselves as well as kangaroo sausage and emu pâté. Sometimes Nick takes off for six day camel safaris along the MacDonnell's. "But today you wouldn't get 'em out for six seconds." In his Reptile House Nick introduced us to the gruesome looking Thorny Devil (*Moloch horridus*), Stimson's python, the blue-tongued lizard and the desert death adder. As he escorted us back to our hire car, passing two bedraggled looking Port Lincoln parrots forlornly sharing an acacia bush, he gain apologised that we weren't getting our camel ride: "Usually it's as dry as a witch's minge. What can you do?"

In the evening we tried to stay sober and cultural with a visit to Starlight Theatreland to listen to modern electrified didgeridoo - Enya in the desert - hypnotic sounds of caterpillars dreaming the MacDonnell Ranges, camels reading the sands and, ominously, rivers in spate. I felt claustrophobic. These were sounds made for the great outdoors, heard under stars and clear skies, not inside a theatre.

Outside it was raining. I thought of the trucker in Douglas Adams' *The Hitchhiker' Guide to the Galaxy* who doesn't know it but he is a rain god and is constantly shocked to find it raining wherever he goes. We popped into the Red Ochre Grill for a wallaby fillet mignon and then, almost inevitably, ended up back in the nastiest pub in town, the Todd Tavern, where various people took to the stage, sung, strummed guitar and were largely ignored before they staggered off again. On the floor, large Australians swore at each other, eyes rolling, stubbed fingers stabbing threateningly in each other's faces and occasionally taking a hopeful swing. One lumbered towards me, stopped momentarily, swaying a foot from my face and grinning inanely. I looked down. Steam was rising from the floor and liquid trickling from his trouser leg. He swayed a little more, shivered and then continued on his journey.

On Sunday we had a wake-up call coming at 5am for a hot air ballooning trip. It didn't come. The receptionist kindly cancelled the call when she saw the rain. "They can't get the pickup truck out through the mud." As we settled our bill, she asked if we were going to the Regatta. "But it was cancelled," I protested. "Yeah well, it's not raining now and they had nothing to do today so they thought bugger it, let's have the regatta anyway." Frantically we tried to switch our flight to the following day but it was fully booked. We were doomed. We had two hours before the flight. Boats were already parading through the mall. Extravagantly decorated Vikings with signs "Kill the women" were dragging "Fuel pack V.B six-packs". We followed them down to the river and just as the first race was about to start, we had to leave. On the way from the enclosure we ran into one of the Rotary members we'd met the day before and he asked why I was going in the wrong direction. I told him how pissed off I was to be missing the Regatta. "No worries," he phlegmatically replied. Most of us miss it and at least you don't have to wake up with a hangover the size of Ayers Rock." His consoling words were probably as sentimental as Alice got.

NDIAN HILL STATION BREAKFAST

The Battle of the Plate

A t Kodai Canal, a hill station in southern India with some 500 resident Brits, we finally find a room in a hotel that appears nameless apart from the legend "Praise be to God" written in the shape of a cross down its five storeys. The hotel has carefully been built in the only noisy spot within a radius of thirty miles and sideways onto the road so you don't have to look at the panoramic view over the valley. Having unpacked, we wade through the Gideon bibles and stride out in search of breakfast.

Venturing into a nearby restaurant, famished, we immediately ask to order. The eminency smiles and asks, "Drinks or food?" Ambitiously, we reply, "Both, if possible." We are given two forms: one green, one yellow. The first, for drinks, we must fill in and submit to another smartly dressed gentleman further down the counter. The second, for food, we hand to someone on the other side of the room who turns out to be either a twin of the first or someone who can move very fast. India took to colonial bureaucracy with a passion that suggests it had always been lying doggo there in the blood waiting for the British to return to Surrey.

My companion has ordered *one plate* of toast, butter and jam. I have ordered two fried eggs and *one plate* of toast and butter. Now you may think *one plate* an odd thing to order, but in India to request, say, four slices could lead to four platefuls containing two, four, or even as here, six slices per plate depending on the individual restaurant's concept of "plate". It is therefore possible to end up with 24 slices of toast. I believe it's all to do with the basic difference between our Euclidian finite mathematical system and the Indian *Palya*, countless base. You have to keep on your toes. Anyway we've ordered carefully and correctly and the drinks quickly follow.

Next, my companion's toast, butter and jam appear independently of each other. I am immediately suspicious. When I'd earlier enquired about the possibility of such an order, I was told, "Toast must be coming butter and jammed." My plan had been to put my two fried eggs on two slices and jam on the other four - it's the kind of project one hatches with another nine months' backpacking ahead and no job to distract from higher meditations.

Two separate plates of single fried eggs arrive next. You never really solve the riddle. Still, no real problem here - I simply uproot one egg and slide it across to join its fellow on the other vintage china plate. Six half-toasted jam sandwiches follow. It's all downhill now. How on earth do they expect me to break an egg over a jam butty? My companion offers me two of her buttered slices. No fork to lift the egg. A young boy appears and tries to take my six jam orphans. I grab the other side of the plate and a tug of war ensues. He wins. My jam butties disappear. I complain at the counter. I want my toast. The two who'd successfully distributed my initial order stride importantly into the kitchen. A huge row breaks out and the two, like sword fighters, emerge battling over the toast, vanish back inside, only to reappear seconds later from another door further up the counter still battling for possession of *the plate*.

My eggs have disappeared beneath a thick coat of congealed grease. I have been forgotten. The plate now has taken on a life of its own. I become hugely irritable. "I want six slices of toast, butter and jam now … and a fork." This halt proceedings. The combatants appear momentarily perplexed but then resume their dispute. It's back to the darkness for me. I look at my eggs. I shout for a fork. Others shout for my fork. The whole of Kodai Canal seems to have involved itself. No fork arrives. I resign myself to my fate, slowly leave the restaurant and return to the hotel room to seek solace in Mr Gideon's wise words that certain mysteries are not meant to be unravelled. No wonder the Indian seeks out non-attachment and extinction.

ACOBSHAVN CORPSES AND THE ARCTIC PLUNGE

Raw seal liver anybody?

On waking that first morning afloat, I pulled back my cabin curtains see a northern fulmar skimming the sleepy waters and beyond it the su blazing above an archipelago of low lying islands. My initial disorientatic was quickly overtaken by excitement. I was finally underway on a new Arct 2,000-plus-mile expeditionary cruise that would explore glaciers and Inu settlements clinging like limpets to the west coast of Greenland, before crossin the Dover Strait to a knuckleduster of rocky outposts constituting the easte boundary of the Canadian Arctic.

Our Greenland adventure commenced with a visit to the vast ice sheet th covers eighty per cent of the world's largest island (a place four times the size France but with the population of Bangor). As I stared slack-jawed into the hu; wall of blinding whiteness at the Russell Glacier, I listened sympathetically its arthritic groans as it edged forever forward. Suddenly an almighty rifle crac disturbed the camera clicking and video whirring as a chunk of 20,000-year-o ice the size of a truck tumbled towards the meltwater to join dozens of simil phantasmagorical ice sculptures scattered like exhibits in a gallery. It felt like drum roll should be sounded to signal the start of my Arctic odyssey.

The Arctic is like the Sahara, a place where everything is reduced to essenc It's a continent, unlike so many others, that can neither be domesticated n reduced to servitude; a place where mountains come to die in polar desert glaciers calve vast orphan icebergs and an ineffable light washes across a da unfathomable sea. In its 5.5 million square miles of emptiness, only the hardie survive.

En route to our second port of call, we passed a cortege of floating sepulchr corpses carved from the Jakobshavn Icefjord drifting in the opposite directior We moored offshore and a fleet of the ship's Zodiacs ferried us across to Ilulissa a town inhabited by 5,000 humans and 6,000 sledge dogs.

In packs of our own, we tramped past a rainbow of clapboard homes and colonial church before setting out on a four-hour hike to a log jam of iceberg calved from the Jacobshavn. Designated a UNESCO World Heritage Site, th was the world's fastest moving glacier, travelling at 46 metres per day in summe months and jettisoning twenty million tons of ice daily into the ocean. It also believed to have been the source of the monster that sank the *Titanic*. It estimated that when, rather than if, the entire Greenland ice sheet melts, it wi result in a global sea level rise of more than seven metres.

Up on a bluff we stood watching the log jam of icebergs 100 metre offshore. Separating us was a narrow skirt of land peppered with the stone an peat remains of Inuit communities that somehow endured here for 2,000 yea by hunting anything that moved - whale, musk ox, seal, arctic fox, birds - an offered sustenance through the cruellest winters on earth.

Now it was summer but the clouds were closing in and rain was gently falling. As we put away our cameras and prepared to leave, nature suddenly demanded our undivided attention once again as one of the huge icebergs imploded as a chasm collapsed with a mighty roar.

Soon we were back on board, sailing across the Davis Strait and entering Canada's newest province, Nunavut. Just off Baffin Island anchored at the incongruously named Monumental Island - a sheer skirt of shattered, glacially scoured gneiss stretching no more than half a mile in length - a message was relayed over the intercom informing kayakers to get into our dry suits.

Foremost in my mind as we commenced paddling through the calm waters was guide Val Lubrick's earlier warning to "maintain a respectful distance from the shore as walrus like to investigate anything unfamiliar with their tusks". Staring up at the barren rock, I'd just concluded it was impossible that anything living could survive here when, rounding a bend, we came upon a polar bear cub nuzzled into a mother who warily watched us slowly drift past. "The calf's around two," Val informed us. "This'll be her last summer with mum. Next year she's on her own." Mum continued to stare for a while at the strange creatures in brightly coloured kayaks and then lost interest, unwilling to expend any unnecessary energy.

Half an hour later, having snaked our way through a narrow inlet, we came upon another polar bear, a male this time, larger, more powerful and less indifferent to our presence as it stood on its hind legs, clearly agitated, rolling its head from side to side. As our presence was disturbing the bear, Val signalled for us to move away.

My heart had only just managed to calm itself when the sea suddenly erupted as a pod of thirty walruses, tusks glistening, heaved themselves in a frenzied pack nearby. Reluctant to be investigated more closely we put on a spurt only to be passed by yet another huge polar bear swimming at a pace that would have left Michael Phelps in its wake.

Between sorties ashore, we attended lectures by the expedition leaders who seemed to collectively boast more PhDs than many universities. The talks focused on everything from glaciology and wildlife to Inuit culture and the doomed expeditions of Europeans seeking the Northwest Passage.

Each day on board was like the first day on earth: the air felt like it had never been breathed before and the boundless ocean shone like lacquered teak. Waking to somewhere new is what draws so many to cruising and in the Arctic that something tends to be epic. One evening, as we prepared for an outdoor barbecue on deck, a pod of pilot whales slipped past like ghosts, barely breaking the surface.

Across the Hudson Strait, at the head of a narrow fjord, we again anchored offshore and were sped ashore on Zodiacs to the small Inuit community of Kimmirut (pop. 411). Here there were no tarmac roads and homes were built to endure rather than titillate. There was a small supermarket, a church, a post office, a school and that was it. Supplies came in by sea twice a year and very few visitors made it out here and so the community understandably made a big fuss of us, guiding us around their town before putting on a show.

Inside a large unadorned hall, two local girls in traditional Inuit costume performed a competitive "throat singing" duet virtually nose-to-nose. The haunting, rhythmic song built and built as each took fast guttural turns inhaling and exhaling sound until one ran out of breath and broke into laughter. It was then time for the boys to show off their athletic prowess competing in games such as knuckle hopping, leg wrestling and head pushing which had clearly been invented to help pass the endless dark winter days with no other equipment but themselves.

Finally it was our turn to join in as we were led outside to a white sheet that had been spread on the ground and on which a freshly killed seal lay indifferent to whatever came next. Above it stood one of the community elders who told us it was always the custom to greet visitors with food. As he crouched, ignoring his complaining knees, he sank a knife into the seal's blubber, filleting it like a kipper. Soon he was proffering slices of raw seal to any of us willing to try. I confess to only managing a sliver which I was relieved to find tasted remarkably like calf's liver.

On our Arctic adventure we encountered humpback, bowhead, beluga and pilot whales; nine polar bears; more than 100 walrus; and countless ringed and bearded seals. We'd pulled into Inuit communities, eaten raw seal and musk ox, kayaked, walked, explored by Zodiac and cruised more than 2,000 miles, mostly in sunshine. It's worth considering these things if you're considering finally trying a cruise and would like more of an adventure than ticking off Caribbean ports.

Our climax came two days before disembarkation. This time it wasn't glacier calving nor bowheads breaching. No, on this occasion we were the wildlife and it was time for those willing to take the traditional end-of-cruise Polar Plunge. I wasn't in the water more than thirty seconds but it sealed my respect for any creature that calls the Arctic its home.

That night, right on cue, the Green Flash visited as the aurora borealis shimmered across the sky. A delirium seemed to take everyone on board and I eventually headed to bed at 3am, leaving many of the crew along with the heavy-partying Chinese still hard at it. My final memory of the bar was of a young marine biologist lashing a middle-aged former Chinese government employee with a leather belt across his bare back as everyone whooped encouragement.

JACOBSHAVN CORPSES AND THE ARCTIC PLUNGE

Fittingly, on our final morning we received the ultimate pilot to lead us to our disembarkation docking at Churchill: wave after wave of Belugas with their calves, frolicking and feeding before heading out for winter once again into the frozen North.

KYPROS

The absent butler and the crazed waiter

When the Thalassa hotel started receiving guests, it greeted holidaymakers with an individual butler to each of its 58 guest "residences" and a catchy slogan to encapsulate the new heady heights of promised service - "The answer is yes, what is the question?"

Pulling into the car park in late October, I expected my bag to be instantly carried and unpacked, my clothes ironed and hung, round-the clock doting attention and someone to clean my teeth. The manager smiled warmly and welcomed us with the boast. "Anyone can get the big things right. It's noticing the small things that make the difference and that is where the Thalassa excels." Unfortunately our butler was nowhere to be seen. Samantha was at Larnaca airport awaiting our arrival despite us telling the hotel we'd be arriving at Paphos. Until Samantha realised her mistake and headed back to the Thalassa, we were to make do with a substitute butler - "An administrative mix up; these things unfortunately do happen from time to time." Marios speedily and efficiently showed to our espresso-making *residence* (the Thalassa has no truck with simple "rooms").

For many less enlightened Cypriot hoteliers, the "big thing" remains the beach but the Thalassa eschewed such petty concerns and located itself on a skirt of ugly rock. One hundred yards north was a noisy and packed curl of sand and to the south a skinny stretch was flanked by builders' rubble.

The hotel did, however, get those "small things" right when it came to tailor-making an individual itinerary such as picnicking on goats cheese and shellfish beneath an almond tree in a vineyard serenaded by a braying donkey. The small thing would appear on your bill at check out at £100 plus.

Samantha was there waiting coolly in the baking heat as we duly approached along a dusty track at around 1.30pm the next day. Our delight at lunching so rustically was tempered by concerns for our butler as she circumnavigated the almond tree, one hand tucked behind her back and the other attempting to serve chilled wine to the appropriate guest in the appropriate order (women first and always from the left) as branches did their best to impale her.

Surprisingly, to master such dexterity, Samantha had needed no special training to become a butler for she had come hotfoot from working in what was then Europe's largest shopping mall, the Bluewater Centre at Gravesend. Like the rest of the fleet, Samantha had, however, been programmed by the management to watch for our tell-tale non-verbal behavioural signals to answer a need before we were even conscious of it. If my arms were resting on the table and my body leaning forward, I was clearly in conversation and shouldn't be interrupted. If I was leaning back and looking around, I may well be seeking the next course.

The flaw in the system soon became apparent back at the hotel when Samantha never seemed to be around to pick up the signals. From breakfast until lunch and lunch until dinner our butler was invisible.

Between coveting others guests' butlers who seemed to provide a steady stream of cold towels and drinks on the hotel terrace, we made the most expansive non-verbal signs imaginable. We stood on our sun loungers making semaphore arm movements that hostesses on Virgin Galactic flights would be able to make out. Eventually we decided to revert to old-fashioned verbal cues but other guests' butlers expertly brushed these aside having been programmed only to deal with their personal clients. Abandoned, we approached the bored looking, unemployed barman but he too insisted we really must go through our butler as "She is here to wait exclusively on you."

Just as the hotel showed suggestive signs of an origin as a planned three star (e.g. the municipal railings on the balconies painted lilac - "the colour of tranquillity") so too the butlers were in reality no more than dressed-up waiters. The real problem, however, was that our waitress was not waiting. We were Samantha was either having a fag round the bike rack or helping with the linen, preparing food in the kitchen or employed in other tasks that butlers need to assist with when they account for virtually the full contingency of staff.

As the lobby had dispensed with a check-in desk ("It really is so passé") anyone wandering in off the street with an enquiry similarly found only ghosts to assist them. When I mentioned our problem to the manager, he claimed that the Thalassa was unusually overburdened with the number of guests currently checked in. We saw five other couples throughout our stay.

Perhaps, just as the simple efficiency of the pencil by rights should have superseded the computer, so too the personal butler is a primitive experiment leading to the waiter, any of whom you can flag down with a request.

On our second evening at the hotel, impatient for dinner at 8.30pm and still with no sign of Samantha, we ferried our own drinks (which we'd forced the barman to reluctantly provide) to our table. Someone - not Samantha - eventually took our order. The swimming pool bubbled aquatically beside closed white umbrellas that looked like sad old tennis skirts in the Wimbledon LT. Museum. Notes cascaded from the piano for guests sitting at the only other three occupied tables. When our main courses arrived they were humble Cypriot dishes – *tavva* and *afelia* twisted into exotic pyramids. The manager, doing his rounds, stopped at our table. "It feels like a liner here doesn't it, heading out to sea?" On our promontory we were indeed surrounded by sea on three sides but if it was a ship, it was the *Mary Celeste*.

Before heading for bed I decided on a late Jacuzzi in the spa. The water was freezing and the pump wouldn't switch on. I made a mental note to ask

Samantha about it the following morning if I could find her. Oh and the fact the air conditioning didn't appear to be working. I'm sure she's a very able plumber.

The next day we checked out and headed over to a more familiar bolthole of ours that I'd been visiting virtually every year since 1979, when, during a four-year teaching stint in Nicosia, I used to call in for a swim and brandy sours after playing football for the mighty Nicosia Nomads against the squaddies at the Episkopi British military base.

As I sat with the sea at my feet and the sun warming my face on the terrace of Kastro's taverna in Pissouri Bay, I let out a mighty sigh and banished all thoughts of the Thalassa. I was back in our second home and as usual being entertained by Xenios, one of four brothers (along with assorted wives, children and parents) who run the taverna. As was his eccentric way, Xenios was at that moment dancing amorously with a broom just as a British couple in matching Bri Nylon outfits appeared on the terrace theatrically flourishing a newspaper in front of them.

"It says in this paper that this is the most authentic taverna in the whole of Cyprus." The woman sounded very pleased with herself rather like Livingstone might have when he finally discovered the source of the Nile.

Xenios peered at the flourished feature and then scowled, "Who wrote that?!" The lady withdrew to the shoulder of her husband before flourishing the article again in front of her like a shield. Xenios peered again. "That fucker. That bloody fucker. Don't believe a word that fucker writes. He writes about us too many times and he's a lying motherfucker. Nothing is true. This place is shit."

The woman, noticing her husband was well behind her now, and keenly aware she was toe to toe to with a lunatic, started backing towards the steps. "It's rubbish here. Don't believe a word." Then Xenios smiled and flourished a plastic menu. "Here. Sit down. Please." Xenios dropped the broom and grabbed the woman's arm and led her to a table. Her husband sheepishly followed. Once they were seated, still ashen faced, Xenios turned and introduced the author of the article who happened to be sitting at the next table. Me. It was a feature I'd written the year before on my last visit to the island.

Kastro's is the kind of place that I'd put money on to be still operating long after the Thallassa runs aground on its petticoat of rocks.

Xenios' father, Costas, in mustard jacket, razor-sharp trousers and highly buffed shoes, sat staring at his youngest son indulgently. He smiled across to me and rolled his eyes before continuing to finger his worry beads like a nun her rosary. Earlier that morning I'd been hunting with him up in the hills when he was dressed in equally dapper fatigues. As a young man doing the rounds in Limassol, Costas had turned heads with his winkle pickers and his waxed moustache. At that time his family were poor farmers. Costas assured me that boys back then, before the tourists arrived, started their amorous live with a donkey for a girlfriend and a stool to assist them. Apparently in those early days the land along the coast was earmarked for the dimmest son in the family as it had little or no value. The best inland agricultural land wa reserved for the brightest. And that is how Costas had come by his prim beach-front plot. Xenios himself had started with a kebab stall on the beach in the late 1970s at the start of the tourist dawn and not long afterwards th family opened Kastro's (so named because Costas was keen on the leader of th Cuban revolution).

Costas had driven us in his 15-year-old pale blue Isuzi pick-up along a dirt road flanked by wild poppies and yellow mimosa to cut the artichoke I was now enjoying on the terrace. En route, between long drags on hi cheroot, he'd sung Cypriot pop songs gustily and told me how in the 1950 and 1960s he'd often bumped along this same dirt road at night in his white winkle pickers to visit a show at one of Limassol's cabaret clubs. "Now we have a motorway and it takes fifteen minutes and the cabarets are full o giant Russian women of easy virtue." He grew a little rueful. "It's life's little joke. When we are young we have no soup, when we are old, we have plenty of soup but no spoon."

Costas spends his days flitting between his fields and the taverna where he works his worry beads, watches TV and goes through several stage costumes a day, never having quite given up his dandyish Limassol days. His wife Maria when she isn't in Jerusalem on another pilgrimage with her sister, works in the kitchen. Sonia, a Bulgarian university graduate who used to teach Russian ("Since '89 there hasn't been much call for Russian"), helps her. To supplemen its own local workforce, Kastro's, like the whole of Cyprus, makes the most o the political and economic upheavals on the three continents at the centre o which it sits. Before Sonia, there was Amara from Sri Lanka and before Amara there was Mohammed from Iran (inexplicably renamed Robert by the family and sacked in 1996 by Xenios - "Nice man but he liked to hide our money in his shoe").

The four generations that daily come and go at Kastro's - Costas, his mothe Urania, Costas' wife Maria, their sons Xenios, Aristos, Leonides and Evagoras and their own wives and children - were my open scrapbook on the changing face of Cyprus.

The sea is a sparkle of fireflies taking nervous dips beneath the soft translucen water as wild, straw-haired David drives up on his 650 Honda, grumbling greetings and heading straight for the fridge to help himself to a large carton of orange juice. In Pissouri there's a burgeoning expat community who have settled, begrudgingly sharing their taverna with the tourists and villagers. Five minutes later, a retired English doctor named Peter arrives for "a large Carlsberg and a belated full breakfast packed with as much grease and carbohydrate as possible please".

The day turns like a spit towards the blinding white of afternoon. Evagoras, the eldest son, arrives from Paphos with a truck load of melons. Once, he informs me, before the valley was planted with vines, the whole area was a sea of watermelons from which a frugal living was scraped, aided by the humble carob and olive. At the age of seven Evagoras was already helping to plough his father's land and by nine had responsibility for two cows.

The parcels of land everyone seemed to own in those days had next to no value. Costas remembers selling one largish tract before the Turkish invasion in 1964 for £900. It was recently resold for £900,000. As children, Evagoras confesses, they often felt hungry living on their diet of potatoes, eggs and artichokes. In those days the family of six squeezed into the two-bedroomed home that Maria and Costas now occupy on their own.

Xenios, the youngest brother, talks of the excitement he carried through the week as a young boy knowing that on Saturday he would go to the village *kafeneion* (coffeehouse) up on the hill. It's still there, bare apart from the elderly sitting at chairs gathering dust and staring vacantly through the television screen into their past. It is hard to imagine anyone being excited about visiting it. "Sometimes the whole family came down to the beach on donkeys from the village for outings. We all looked forward to it and Easter and Christmas were the bedposts of the year. Now every day is Christmas - everything is available every day and the days cannot be divided."

Somehow, somewhere along the way Xenios, like his older brothers, feels something got lost. Innocence perhaps. Eventually tourism was discovered and Costas and the boys embraced it. Though nostalgic for the old ways, each son, however, is glad to be offering his own children more than their mother and father could offer them growing up. Evagoras' eldest daughter is a gold medal student in Limassol who has won study trips to Paris and Athens and has plans to become a translator. He is very proud of her but would dearly like his daughters to remain in the village and his son work the land with him.

Like all Cypriots, the brothers do several jobs simultaneously. Evagoras works for the water board in Limassol, cultivates his vines and helps with the restaurant. Xenios hires out jet skis and umbrellas. Both he and Evagoras now also own self-catering apartments and villas which they let to tourists. Leonides, the third brother, rarely appears in the taverna - he's too busy running his own bar (Sparti) in the village. Aristos, the fourth, meanwhile, escapes with his nine-year-old son to his 85-acre farm every minute he can. The ninety sheep, vines and olives don't yield much of a return (about £2,500 a year profit) but he'd probably do it for nothing. "The sheep all eat the same - they don't ask for mezes," he explains.

As the day continues to turn, Evagoras leaves, Aristos arrives with daughter Elli, Costas changes outfit again and Lynn, originally from Staffordshire and now living in the next village, takes over with Aristos' wife, Georgina, in the kitchen. Like the raindrops of pure light that dance on the sea, guilelessly Kastro's provides all that is memorable about the island and reminds me of why I keep coming back. The Thalassa has been erased like a bad dream.

By 6pm the scorch has gone from the day. Swallows fight like swashbucklers above the olive trees. The sky turns copper and finally provides a fuel tank explosion at sea. By 10pm my own endless meze is disappearing as is the last of the carafe of wine from Evagoras' vines. I ask for a toothpick and Aristos steps outside to cut me one from a tree. Xenios meanwhile is regaling me with hilarious tales from his conscript days in the army before he ran away. All the brothers are witty but Xenios is undoubtedly the star. When I ask him why the two English children aged around nine are eating here alone, he replies, "They're on honeymoon." Earlier, when someone asks what the Cypriot special of the day is, quick as a flash he answers, "Egg and chips." When someone else enquires about his 92-year-old grandmother's health, Xenios replies, "Much better... She just doesn't know who her grandson is."

Xenios, like his brothers, share friendship - the greatest strength of Cypriot tourism - with regulars and newcomers alike, pulling up a chair, offering cigarettes, joking and bitching about life.

When, finally, Xenios' six-year-old daughter Teresa asks to be taken home, he exits in a parodic Zorba dance, again with the broom, to an exaggerated bazooki trill. Next it is time for Elli, Aristos' 14-year-old daughter, to depart for home and bed. She comes round to each table to bid goodnight to every customer. The extended family is alive and well and living in Cyprus. Aristos brings over another carafe of wine and we switch tables to get closer to the gentle surf rolling in beneath the stars.

LYING DOGGO

Out of air in Africa and the Himalayas

Sitting in the hotel bar back in Paro, the conversation suddenly ran out of steam. The usual sense of triumph and exhilaration at having completed a sixteen-day trek in the Himalayas was tempered by the knowledge that the party was one short. On October 16, four days earlier, at the age of 46, the youngest in the group had died suddenly of acute mountain sickness (AMS).

Having just completed my own Bhutanese trek, I happened to be sitting in the same bar listening to the group as they attempted to reassure their leader that he had done all he could. He thanked them for their kindness and left the bar to sort out the deceased's personal effects. The trek leader was clearly experienced, attentive and thorough. So why did one of his party die?

I had first-hand experience of just how easy it could be. On Mount Kenya, a decade earlier, I'd come within a hair's breadth of a similar exit. Prior to my Kenyan jaunt, I'd trekked in Europe, the Andes, New Zealand and five times in Nepal. I was an old hand and had never experienced any problems with altitude. For the Mount Kenya trek, however, I'd flown overnight from London and then driven six hours to the Chogoria Gate at 10,000 feet. My fellow trekkers had already been in the country three days acclimatising. I started with a headache and things got worse. But I was lucky; it could have got much worse - a week before my visit an Irishman had died of a pulmonary embolism on the same trek. I believe it was due to a chance encounter with a Swiss medic that I didn't follow him.

The first and most humbling thing to know about AMS is that it can hit anyone regardless of age or fitness. The second, and most important thing to know is if it does hit, get down the mountain fast. The Irish doctor was in a party of medics and yet they made the fatal mistake of trying to medicate him rather than make him descend and he paid the ultimate price.

My introduction to AMS came while I was sitting on a toadstool-shaped rock perched on an overhang with a 300-foot sheer drop below me. Suddenly I started to feel dizzy. We were a little less than twenty miles from the equator and it was just after midday. The headache that had been pounding to get in for a several days seemed to have taken over my entire body. I took another swig from my water bottle and started the descent, keeping as close to Sammy, our guide, as possible. The gorge we were descending became a hallucinatory vortex of gargantuan carnivorous-looking plants, rainbow-coloured rocks and cascading water. At the base, skirting a dazzling lake, was an army of ten-foot high lobelia. I concentrated - it was precipitous and slippery and the scree at the base was still 200 feet away.

When I finally reached the banks of Lake Michaelson my body went into spasm and I vomited. Sammy sat me down, made me drink a litre of warm tea and packed me off to my tent. I would spend the next thirteen hours in and out of my sleeping bag alternating drinking from the thermos Sammy kept refilling, and peeing.

I slept fitfully. At one point, listening to blood pounding in my temple, I remember cursing Sean who I could hear praying too loudly as usual in the next tent. Sean had been born deaf and had no awareness of volume.

The next morning I rose early and stood chatting with our cook while he prepared porridge, sausages and omelettes for David, Joe, Brenda and Sean. I stuck with biscuits and more tea. Over breakfast Sean mentioned he'd been praying for me during the night. I felt a little guilty at having cursed him. Just a little. "It worked too, didn't it Paul? Now do you believe?" I liked Sean. He had no sides to him and, standing six foot four, was built like a Yeti. He had climbed in the Alps and his ambition was to be the first deaf man up Everest. No, I still didn't believe, but I was grateful to anyone who'd tried to extricate me from the hell-hole I'd been in the night before. Sammy meanwhile had taken over from Ruud Gullit as my hero.

Today the sun was shining. We were breakfasting next to a lake the colour of jade flanked by giant lobelia and wraparound mountains; and, as with our previous overnight camp at Lake Ellis, we only had to share the beauty with each other. Life was good again.

Our trek had begun two days earlier at the Meru Park Gate where a sign had baldly warned, "Wild animals. Stay on track, be audible and yield the right of way." Wheatears had flickered above grass dappled with wild scabious like the corn fields back home, but here the ground was also dotted with the dung of elephant, zebra and eland. Soon the groves of bamboo that creaked in the breeze like old men's knees gave way to savannah. A string of lakes appeared and occasionally I caught the smell of wild thyme and the pungent curry plant. On one occasion, with plumes of fine red dust puffing up from our boots, we skirted a cortege of buffalo making to graze in the scrub.

Towards the end of that first day's trek, we'd cut across tussock grass and hiked to the top of the Giant's Billiard Table, a volcanic plug, where we had our first clear view of Mount Kenya itself, surprisingly soft and downy but topped by a finial of forbidding peaks.

After dinner at our Lake Ellis base that night, I'd wandered across to join the crew who were standing around their camp fire beneath a sky packed with a billion pinprick stars. The temperature plummets as quickly as nightfall on the equator. We stood in the bowl that cradled the lake, staring up at the black-thumbed outline of Kenya's highest peak (Kilimanjaro's is strictly speaking in Tanzania). We poked sticks in the fire creating a comet shower, and rotated occasionally to warm our backsides as talk turned to Ripleys-Believe-It-Or-Not stories of extraordinary feats and extraordinary people. I remembered similar nights as a boy around camp fires in Wiltshire swapping with my brother tales of the Dagon people, Saharan Tuaregs and Hindu fakirs. Now, as then, as our

stories grew more fantastic, they collided with deep primordial fears. And for m
African companions, the deepest fear was not lions nor elephants but snakes.

As I was about to turn in, Ali sidled up to me and, probably believin
he was exorcising my dreams, whispered conspiratorially, "Don't worry abou
snakes, Paul. Sometimes lions can be a problem migrating over the mountain
a German, camping near the Met station, was woken three years ago by a lio
tearing his leg off - but there are no snakes up here."

Despite the stories, I did sleep. But coincidentally the next morning
during a pre-breakfast stroll, I came across a snake's eighteen-inch slougher
skin. I decided to take it back to camp for identification. Everybody shied away
perhaps it was a bad omen like they said an owl on a rooftop was.

After breakfast, we broke camp, skirted Lake Ellis, passing four eland grazin
in the distance, and began following a six-inch wide trail upwards through shin
high tussock grass, African heather and lichen-stained rocks. As we climbed
we began to notice that it was not only the peaks that were growing bigger bu
the plant life too was undergoing a process known as "gigantism" whereby th
flora and foliage grows to prodigious sizes because nature here experiences both
winter and summer seasons every 24 hours.

At around 2pm I found myself on the escarpment I mentioned at th
beginning of my tale, perched on that toadstool-shaped rock 300 feet abov
Lake Michaelson. Across on the far hillside something was sparkling in the roc
face like gneiss. "It's the debris from a crashed plane," Sammy explained. It wa
then that I started feeling dizzy. My headache had undergone its own gigantism
I knew we would be sleeping down by the lakeside at a lower altitude than w
were now. If I could just get down and rest, I was sure I'd be fine. Somehow
made it ... and then fell apart. Altitude sickness had taken my legs, turned m
insides out and squeezed my head in a vice so tight that the headache had taker
over my body.

But after thirteen hours of rehydration and recuperation I now felt ready
for our hardest day's walk. Today we would leave Lake Michaelson and ascend
1,700 feet to the Tooth, a high pass into the coronet of Mount Kenya's highes
peaks. Here we would overnight at Austrian Hut (15,700 feet) before making a
pre-dawn trek up the final 650 feet to Point Lenana.

Sammy advised caution. "Take it very slowly, Paul. The air's thin, you're or
the equator and it's a long climb. Remember to keep drinking. If the sicknes:
returns and gets very bad, you have no choice, you must descend." It was then
that he told me about the Irish doctor who had died the week before of a
pulmonary embolism.

Despite the shock of Sammy's revelation, I felt so fully recovered that I
couldn't wait to get walking again. Ironically it was my fellow walkers David and

Joe who were feeling the worse for wear. David said he felt as if he had flu: Joe simply confessed to "feeling like shit". Neither had slept. Brenda and Sean, who made up the party, appeared to still be in fine fettle.

As we broke camp and started our slow ascent, my feeling of elation returned. The climb was steep but, taken slowly, manageable. The views were staggering with hanging valleys, tarns, snow-splashed peaks and tumbling streams that had formed ice overhangs on rocks. Today we were in the southern hemisphere. Tomorrow we would walk into the northern hemisphere. If someone wasn't exhilarated here, they must already, surely, be dead.

For much of the morning I walked with Moses, a gentle giant who served as our second guide. After a while discussing our respective home lives, conversation turned to Mount Kenya's tallest peaks, Batian (17,050 feet) and Nelion (17,020 feet), which we were constantly closing on. "Many people still believe God lives up there," Moses informed me pointing vaguely in the direction of Batian before telling me of a local farmer who recently had to be rescued from the peaks when he used ropes left by previous expeditions to climb up it to pray. When Bongo Woodley, the Mount Kenya National Park warden, got him down he warned, "Don't you ever come into the park again without permission." Cooly the man replied, "I'll come when I want." Moses laughed and told me the farmer, who lived near his own village, was planning to return soon to pray some more.

As our own ascent became more acute, conversation was ditched as every gasp for air had to be fought for. We finally reached the top of the Tooth (15,500 feet) around 2pm and followed a gentle traverse above a tarn on the final 200-foot climb to our overnight base at Austrian Camp.

During the ascent I had fared reasonably well but on stopping, a wave of nausea again swept through me. A fist seemed to be pressing into my chest and I was gasping for air. I drank two plastic mugs of tea and lay down on my sleeping bag squeezed between three other resting bodies on the wooden floor.

Instead of improving, my breathing worsened and I started to shake. Sammy instructed me to get inside the sleeping bag to get warm. I drank another litre of warm tea but I was still grabbing for air and felt overwhelmingly tired. Sleep seductively tugged at me, but each time I started to drift down to it, some hypothalamic reaction snapped me back. As one falls asleep, breathing slows and I already wasn't getting enough air; I feared that if I succumbed, I would lose consciousness and never regain it. I thought of the Irishman who'd died the week before. My body was now in spasm and the fist in my chest was nearly through to the other side.

A Swiss mountaineer and doctor who was about to descend 1,500 feet to Mackinder's Camp with a colleague, also suffering altitude sickness, took one look at me and insisted I too descend. Sammy concurred and quickly gathered up my belongings. In a daze, I descended the precipitous scree. One slip and there was nothing between me and the valley floor. I moved painfully slowly, still feeling desperate for sleep, but as we descended, I felt the fist loosen.

Eventually we emerged round the back of Mount Kenya. Sammy and I were now on the Naro Moru side and I stared up at the terrifying beauty of the Diamond Couloir running sheer from the Gate of Mist between the twin gnarled peaks of Batian and Nelion.

It took over an hour to descend and another hour to cross a bog and follow the valley out to Mackinder's Camp where Sammy and I would spend the night, and where the rest of the party would rejoin us the following morning.

By the time we arrived at Mackinder's, the sickness had lifted like a fog. There were three others staying in the dorm who had been forced to descend for similar reasons. All three, surprisingly, were mountaineers. As I chatted into the night with Sammy and the others beside the burr of a hurricane lamp, someone suddenly shone a torch out of the window and there sitting ten feet from us was a two-foot tall, rarely-spotted Mackinder's Eagle Owl staring back at us from a rock. I remembered what Moses had told me earlier in the trek about owls on rooftops being auguries of a family death. The owl fortunately remained rooted to the rock.

In the morning I felt enormously sorry for myself as I sat on my own rock beside a stream, staring up at Point Lenana which I could just make out above the Diamond Couloir and which the rest of my friends would now be ascending. Eventually, however, gazing into the ice fields and bare upper mountain peaks that defied anything to cling them, I realised how lucky I was to be here. I felt well, had trekked through glorious countryside and had even had a close encounter with a Mackinder's Eagle Owl. Now a hyrax was scuttling by - cat-sized, trilling like a bird, looking like a tail-less beaver and closest relative, preposterously, to the elephant. A brilliant green malachite sunbird balanced on a tree, its eight-inch tail seemingly performing an independent war dance below the branch. A hill chat skipped to within six inches of me. Birds simply had no fear of humans here and now I had nothing to fear either.

It struck me I could look at my trek one of two ways: either it was a failure because I'd missed the last 600 feet up to Point Lenana; or it was a success simply because I'd walked up a three-million-year-old mountain in Africa. How on earth could I feel cheated?

When the rest of the party caught up with us around 11am Brenda looked like a zombie and David worse. He told me he'd endured the worst night of his life. "When you quit the hut, the clenched fist moved in with me." David hadn't slept a wink and confessed, "If it hadn't been pitch dark and so treacherous, I would have followed you down." Joe was limping from the high-impact descent nd thought his head was going to explode. Sean, however, was still in galloping mode: "Why do we want to go down? It's lovely up there in the mountains and 's crap down there."

We still had a final four-hour walk ahead to the bizarre Vertical Bog and its gravity-defying giant groundsel and lobelia. At the track-head, we made camp or the last time at the Met Station next to a party from an international Seventh Day Adventist college in Nairobi. As I lay resting in my tent that evening, I listened to their group leader preparing them for the mountain and trying to instil in them respect for it. As they formed a circle round him on the grass, he attempted to provide a sense of scale. "Travelling at the speed of light it would take you 1/60th of a second to get from Los Angeles to New York and eight minutes to reach the sun and yet our own galaxy alone is 120,000 light years across." Six hundred feet did not seem such a big deal put like that.

For several years after Mount Kenya I avoided trekking beyond 10,000 feet, but then the lure of the Himalayas became a stronger pull than my fears. Surely it wouldn't happen again. After all, it had never happened before. The likelihood was my Mount Kenya experience was simply down to my lack of acclimatisation.

This time we treked in Sikkim, an unspoilt north-eastern Indian corner bordering Tibet, Bhutan, Nepal and the populous Indian state of West Bengal. And this time I played by the rules, spending three days in Darjeeling acclimatising. Seven days into the trek, however, I felt the first signs that the ghosts of Mount Kenya had caught up with me and were now stalking my every step.

The previous day's trek, named "Execution Day" by our lead Sherpa, had been tough. We'd trudged vertically for nine hours, sucking hard at the thin Sikkim air as we ascended 4,260 feet between camps.

Somehow, despite my exhaustion and my body feeling like death the next morning, I managed to crawl out my sleeping bag to make the 4am reveille and ascend once more through the snow, my equally feeble torch picking out the route ahead. Eventually we reached Dzonghi Top (13,500 feet), the climax of the trek, where we'd been promised close-up views of the world's third highest mountain, Kangchandzonga (28,166 feet).

Amazingly we found that despite being in the middle of nowhere and several days from any road, four other trekkers, had beaten us to it and were hopping from foot to foot trying to prevent their toes from freezing. We joined them, chatting, hopping and waiting expectantly.

After twenty minutes, the moment we'd been waiting for finally arrived as the sun coyly peeked over the world's mightiest mountain range and then opened like a fan, gilding the Himalayan peaks before racing down the Rathong Glacier. Eight snowy peaks almost 20,000 feet rose like white-robed priests.

Down below us in the other direction, slumbering in the valley's penumbra, lay the puny blue tented peaks of our overnight camp where an hour later my seven friends and I would hopefully be back toasting our fine Himalayan dawn over breakfast hot chocolate.

Taking a risk to get that close to heaven almost inevitably means having to spend a little time in hell too; along with the great days just about everyone has one they'd sooner forget and this was mine. The dizziness, the vomiting, the exploding head returned.

The following day my friend Dave from the Kenya trek had his worst moment. When crossing a tree trunk bridge across a stream, as the group returned from Lake Semity in gently falling snow, suddenly the log rolled, flinging Dave into the rock-strewn stream. His head managed to steer a route between the boulders but he still ended up breaking a finger, bruising a rib, getting soaked and suffering hypothermia.

I meanwhile had remained in camp alternately vomiting and nursing my headache. As the team trudged into camp and wrapped Dave in his sleeping bag once they'd removed his wet clothes, attention turned to Will whose own AMS was manifesting itself by his head and neck swelling to the size of Elephant Man. Bruce too was suffering but not as badly. Altitude sickness may not have the same cachet as some other exotic illnesses but once you've had it, it's hard to imagine anything more hellish. I've sworn to my wife I'll never again go above 10,000 feet.

I am, however, desperate to trek to Ras Dashen in Ethiopia (14,927 feet).

MISSISSIPPI MUSICAL CRADLE

The Devil has the best songs

In the beginning was Elvis. I was eight. We'd just landed in Singapore to join my father - a sergeant in the Royal Artillery - after a three-day flight aboard a Hercules military aircraft. Dad, whose short-sleeved military shirt stuck to his back in the steamy heat, handed me a large case. He told me it contained a machine gun. When I got to the hotel and raised the lid I discovered an acoustic guitar. My first guitar. The guitar slept with me, went to the bathroom with me and more frequently rocked with me in front of the mirror to Elvis' "Hound Dog". I spent months imitating his hip thrusts, curling my lip, smiling with my nose.

When I was twelve and living in Liverpool, an unknown group released a record "Love Me Do". As my mum worked with the drummer's fiancée at Richmond Sausage Works, I decided to donate my saved pocket money to them as they were almost family.

That Saturday, however, on Lime Street Station a wail, like that of a wolf in an animal trap, froze me in my tracks. It was Howlin' Wolf, the man who raised the howl to sacerdotal heights. I left with my first compilation blues album (*Blues Volume Two*) instead of "Love Me Do". I'd lost my musical virginity but kept it secret from my parents, knowing anything that powerful could not possibly be approved of.

Lester Bohren felt similar misgivings as a boy in Wyoming, but made the mistake of trying to share his passion with his Baptist preacher daddy. His father accused him of listening to the Devil's music and threw his records in the bin. So Lester started playing the music himself.

I caught Lester's set in the Snug Harbour club when sheltering from a New Orleans electric storm writing its musical score across a sky so thick you could stand an alligator up in it.

I was finally making my pilgrimage to Louisiana, Mississippi and Tennessee and I was starting it in the city where African slaves once danced in Congo Square and where mannish boys and voodoo children still lived. It was here in "The Town That Care Forgot" that Buddy Bolden invented jazz and then spent thirty years in an insane asylum, where Anne Rice wrote her *Interview with a Vampire* and Tennessee Williams was told to "take a streetcar named Desire, transfer to one called Cemetery and get off at Elysian Fields".

Lester's set was billed as Delta Blues. It was polished and technically flawless, but the voice did not belong to the haunted souls I'd shared my teenage years with. In one song Bohren sang about Natchez - "the prettiest town in Mississippi", where I would be heading next on my 500-mile drive to Memphis along the banks of the world's third largest river. En route I hoped to meet the real Delta bluesmen. Before I left town, however, there was time to squeeze in a second set at the House of Blues where I watched a funky old-style R&B band with Bernie Cyrus, local guitarist and director of the Louisiana Music Commission.

Cyrus was justly proud of his city. "Memphis claims to have invented rock'n'roll but Roy Brown released 'Good Rocking Tonight' here in 1948 - six years ahead of Elvis' first hit." The city had also invented jazz. "Buddy Bolden started it, Jelly Roll polished it and Fats Domino lived it." Warming to his theme, Cyrus even claimed the Liverpool sound originated in New Orleans. "Three of the Beatles' earliest recordings were first cut by Larry Williams in New Orleans 'Dizzy Miss Lizzy', 'Slow Down' and 'Mercy, Mercy, Mercy'."

Cyrus was just one of a host of warm, friendly people I met in the city. There was Pat who guided visitors round free of charge simply because she liked doing it and whose husband still said grace in French and argued with anyone who called New Orleans an American city. There was Don Marquis, knee-deep in boxes at the jazz archives, reminiscing over a meeting with Satchmo when he was nineteen. There was the elderly gentleman I met beneath a statue of General Lee who explained the reason the Confederate leader was pointing towards the YMCA was because the initials stood for "The Yankees May Come Again" ("An' if they do, he'll climb down from his perch and chase 'em straight back the way they came"). Then there was Esther, a psychic healer, and Monica, a business student I met at the Voodoo Museum who earned spare cash as a snake dancer at voodoo rituals.

Not everyone in town likes voodoo. Some Baptists put a lock on the door of the Museum recently, less than happy about the animal sacrifices routinely practised at a temple out on Rampart. The year before Daagbo Hounon, the pope of Voodoo in Benin, visited and even he talked ominously about the disunity in New Orleans' voodoo church. But he still loved haring around the city in a Mazda sports car with his robes flying.

Some New Orleanians may not like it, but they certainly take the cult seriously. Even the city's policemen are rumoured to carry gris-gris (voodoo charms) for protection. The 25-year-old Voodoo Museum sells hexes and unhexes by the coffinload, its cemetery tours are always sold out and during its ever popular night rituals everyone wants to touch Zombie, a 140lb python it takes three to lift.

After three nights in New Orleans, I drove out on Interstate 10 past swamps and the ocean that is Lake Pontchartrain. At Baton Rouge (where my early hero Buddy Guy lived), I swapped Louisiana for Mississippi and headed north on the single-lane Highway 61. Giant magnolias (the state flower) and cypresses started appearing, along with clapboard Baptist churches, aluminium silos and the bleached bones of abandoned shacks. I was now on The Great River Road and as I switched between the "Hang Out With Jesus" radio station and Baton Rouge's "Classic Soul" ("S-s-s-soul never s-s-s-sounded s-so good"), roadway signs tempted me with promises of grilled catfish sandwiches and ali-bobs (alligator-tail kebabs).

Lester was right about Natchez being the prettiest town in Mississippi. Scarlet O'Hara ante-bellum pre-Civil War mansions curtsied from the banks of the mighty river (there are more here than anywhere else in America), paddle steamers trundled and Confederate flags fluttered. I quickly discovered that, like most towns on the Mississippi, however, apartheid still operated wherever possible - nothing caused a bigger furore than when the main street was renamed Martin Luther King Junior Street. Knowing music was the one place racism found it tough to flourish, I headed to a bar named Under the Hill where I'd heard Jerry Lee Lewis used to beat up the piano back in the 1950s.

The piano was still there and so was Andree, the original owner, polishing glasses opposite wooden shutters that stared out on to the great enamelled belly of the river. The bar itself stretched virtually the whole length of the building and on the walls, amid photographs of musicians who'd played here, was one quintessential pose of the wild man of rock combing his hair, aged maybe twenty years old. Andree smiled. "I used to offer him a beer to stop playing, but it did no good; he just kept hammerin' the piano through the floorboards. Jerry was wild, like all them Lewises." He paused and then, fearing I might get the wrong impression, added, "He wasn't bad … just a little crazy. Sure he shot a couple people and beat up a few women, but hell, who hasn't?"

Also on the wall was a trumpet belonging to local jazz musician James Rowan, now aged seventy and who, fortuitously for me, had just popped in to pick up some records somebody had left for him. James' fifteen minutes of fame had come playing King Oliver, Louis Armstrong's mentor, in a musical on Satchmo's life that toured the States. To pay bills between gigs he taught the trumpet and ran bands in local schools. I asked James why he thought the Delta had produced so many great artists. "'Cos people was poor and had nothing. They just kept the blues with 'em all day. They had no one to tell it to so they sung it, an' singin' it made things feel a bit better - a bittersweet thing."

Through James I learnt about the town's best-known bluesman, Jimmy Anderson, whom I finally tracked down at the local jail as he was finishing his shift as lollipop man and security guard at the adjacent school. He invited me into one of station's interview rooms and we sat chatting over cups of coffee under mugshots of the most wanted. Jimmy got his first harmonica at nine and started playing like Little Walter. When he got his first guitar aged seventeen, he took up a Jimmy Reed style and went on the road. He had toured Europe with the Mojo Blues Band four times. He had also recorded eighteen singles and two CDs but admitted, "You cainnn't find none of 'erm nowhere, no mowwwrre." Like virtually every other bluesman, he had to scrape a living outside music. Jimmy made me a tape of his songs and I played it - back-to-back driving up the Great River Road the following day en route to the Delta Blues Festival.

That night I watched the Red Clay Roadhouse Band playing from the back a parked truck as the late sun raked the flanking aluminium storage tanks of e Southern Cotton Oil Company in Greenville. Wolf Man growled through Born under a Bad Sign" as Edwin Holt soared past him on his Gibson. I was e of just two whites in a crowd that had turned up for an appetiser open-air g on Nelson Street.

The following day, in a field a few miles south, the real action - the 19th annual Iississippi Delta Blues and Heritage Festival - would take place, but for those on elson Street, the party was already cranking up. Old men, faces chiselled from coal, nced with grandchildren who'd barely mastered walking. Overweight middle-aged omen strutted alone and didn't give a damn. Standing next to me was a mountain a man in white snakeskin boots, blue jeans and a colourful cap. Aman Hussain, former professional wrestler and originally from Sudan, worked at Perry's Flowing untain, "making damn sure none of the nasties get in: the crack heads, pimps and aight crazies". Sonny Boy Williamson was "a good friend," he claimed, like Muddy aters and Howlin' Wolf, all Mississippi boys now in the grave. He also knew Tina irner when she used to play the Fountain for fifty cents admission.

I was now in the heart of the Delta cotton-picking country and the real me of popular music. Posters on the streets for the festival declared, "If you ven't been to the Delta Blues and Heritage Festival, then you've never been me." It had taken me a while but finally I'd got here.

Dad had given me that first guitar when I was eight; four years later I saved and bought my one and only harmonica - the classic Hohner Super Vamp - ter hearing Little Walter's "Juke". Another year passed and I joined Muddy into e electric age, with a third-hand beat-up Fender. Two more guitars followed as moved from my blues phase to R&B and my final resting place in the bosom soul. I never learned to play a note and sang like a drain.

I had everything the other white boys similarly dreaming in Winchester, verpool and Epsom to the scratched sounds on their box record players had. e only difference between me and the fledgling Yardbirds, Mojos, Bluesbreakers d Rolling Stones was that I had absolutely no talent.

Eventually I sloughed the dream as I did a winner's medal at Wembley. it I never lost my passion for the music and the mystery of these black artists ho so magnificently endured their hostile earth. I'd had to leave it to Blind mon Jefferson and other Delta bluesmen to express so perfectly my pubescent arnings ("I'm broke and I'm hungry, ragged and dirty too. What I want to now sweet mama is can I go home with you?").

The veteran bluesman Willie Foster explained my tragic failure the following y at the festival's Juke House stage: "Only those who really suffer get rewarded th the blues."

Willie had grown up on a local cotton plantation and was sitting in wheelchair signing autographs for forty- to fifty-year-olds with grey moustache and prodigious girths. Willie, now 75, had acquired his first harmonica - also Hohner - aged seven, but unlike me he could really play the thing.

He pulled one of his mouth harps out of a special belt containing six mo which he wore around his dungarees. The wood had darkened and the met plates were worn so smooth from handling that the brand name was no longe visible. "Cost me 25 cents, and I had to save up cotton money two weeks to bu it," Willie grinned.

When I asked who taught him to play, his wrinkled face broke into deep smiling gullies. "A feelin' did... I had the hungry blues, the sick blues, the har workin' blues an' the love blues. They all just tumbled out."

Willie pushed himself out of his wheelchair and moved awkwardly to th small stage, shuffling his "spent legs" and pushing back the crowd like a boa parts water. He sat on the edge of the stage and selected another harmonic from the belt. As the band kicked in, Willie's mouth harp began wailing like coyote and when it left his lips, a voice as murky as the Mississippi, as dark an bottomless as his old friend Muddy Waters (who he'd toured with back in 195; boomed out.

It was the same voice he'd used earlier to demonstrate to me the differenc between Delta Blues and what is served up in Chicago. First he minced h voice effetely into a twangy rubber band and sang fast R&B time. "My bab gowwwwwn an' left me." Then the phrasing slowed and another voice hollere out the pain. One moved your feet, the other moved your soul.

Willie was one of six acts playing the twelve-foot wide stage at the Juk House. There were no seats. A small awning did its best to protect around thir of us from the sun. The rest baked. The Juke House was where traditional har core bluesmen and a couple of the raunchier R&B acts played. It was also wher I spent most of the day.

Bigger acts, such as Tyrone Davis, Denise LaSalle and Vernon Garret played to the larger audience at the main stage. But here too, the best set cam from a local act, the Jerry Kattawar Band. Jerry, a third-generation American o Lebanese origin who daylighted in a truck-rental business, hammered boogi woogies out of his piano with his hands, his feet and his head; stomping th floorboards and leaping like a monkey onto the piano before dancing manical along the keyboard.

Watching Jerry, it became clear why some Baptist choirs had refused perform in the Gospel Tent that had been introduced the year before. Ever sin Robert Johnson sold his soul to Satan in exchange for guitar mastery down at th Crossroads, the blues had been known as the Devil's music.

The Gospel Tent was the only alcohol-free zone at the festival, but when I visited, everyone was drunk on Jesus. The crowd swayed. The choir, dressed in t-shirts emblazoned with the word "Christ", echoed the preacher who worked everyone into a frenzy with his looping litany: "They got some blues out there, what they need is Jeeesuzzzz… They got some Budweiser out there, what they need is Jeeesuzzzz…" Clearly, he too must have been in need of something because after fifteen minutes he passed out.

Outside the tent, flesh was already grilling pink in the sun. A couple had fallen asleep on a pyre of about thirty Bud cans, hugging the last two to their chests. Skirting the field, stalls offered Polish sausages, red beans and rice, chitterlings (aka chitlins - hog intestines) and even whole roasted pigs with crushed beer cans between their teeth. From this banquet, I chose ali-bobs - kebab-sized chunks of alligator tail marinated in Cajun spices, served on a skewer and tasting like tandoori chicken.

At the ali-bob stall I chatted to Bill Seratt, who'd returned to Greenville after a decade away. "The festival's got whiter – probably sixty per cent white now. When I left it was no more than twenty per cent." He ran his fingers through his thinning hair. "Got a lot younger too; unless it's just me getting older."

As the sun dipped behind the main stage, the litter carpet moved up past our ankles. Beside the tents and awnings, garden chairs had been pitched, cool boxes fetched and the crowd had settled into the long, mellow day.

I adjourned to a small hill and a graveyard of discarded animal bones that overlooked the Juke House stage. Here I shared more beers with an extended family that ranged in age from two (Sonny) to 72 (Moses). It was Moses who suggested I head down to the Flowing Fountain a little later as that was where local bands would be playing when they finished their festival sets.

Driving back through Greenville, it was transparently clear that the town remained hopelessly poor. Unemployment was high and the impecunious fate of the majority of its citizens was heightened by the bevy of floating casinos tethered at the levee. Old men sat on porches but no one was picking beaten-up guitars or playing mouth harp. Something had been sucked out of them.

Greenville was home to the bluesman Little Milton. It was also where Elvis sent his private jet for hot tamales from Doe's Eat Place (it's still there and serves four-pound sirloins too). Apart from these two claims to fame, Greenville was just another cotton town on the old blues chitlin' circuit (so named because musicians played for a plate of chitterlings).

Despite the fact that it had played midwife to the world's most influential twentieth-century musical form, and hosted the annual blues festival, there were no other signs of the blues legacy apart from Perry's Flowing Fountain which had been hosting acts for thirty years.

When I arrived, Aman was on the door and Jerry Kattawar was inside abusing his piano some more. Ninety-five per cent of the audience was black, aged between 21 and about 121, and they came in all sizes. I could not remember ever being in a more chilled club. Everybody was too busy having a good time to worry about anything else.

Jerry gave way to the OV Wright Band, led by another local boy, who played steamier, Chicago-style R&B. First a thirty-year-old, then a sixty-year-old woman asked me to dance. Couples older than my parents were engaged in dirty dancing, whose steps were of secondary importance to enthusiastic bumping and grinding.

OV Wright stirred the erotic cocktail, singing: "Anybody here tonight with somebody else's somebody?" He repeated it three times. We could have been back in the Gospel Tent. Unlike the preacher, however, after several repeated questions designed to heighten the sexual frisson, his own delayed answer came: "Well that's all right."

Gospel had heaven and the blues had hell. Well that was all right with me too.

The next day I arrived in Clarksdale with a thick head just as James Super Chikan Johnson and the Fighting Cocks were kicking into their first number at the Delta Blues Museum. John Ruskin, the museum curator, was on keyboards. Among other notable achievements in his young life was a 2,350 mile solo journey on a raft down the Mississippi. Mr Toby on bass was dressed in farmworker dungarees and frontman Jimmy Johnson only removed his pipe when he had to sing.

On a wall behind the band was a diddy-bow like the ones on which Muddy Waters, BB King and Bo Diddley first learnt to play music - primitive slide guitar consisting of a single string pulled taut between two stones on a wooden plank and played with a third stone. As Ruskin later explained, "People were so poor they made instruments from anything. Our local barber, Wade Walton, is still known as 'The Blues Barber of Clarksdale' 'cos for forty years he's been playing blues on his razor strap to customers like Muddy and Sonny Boy."

As the band swung into "Hoochie Coochie Man", I wandered round the museum. There were early posters, blues tomes, thousands of CDs and tapes and 500 videos of Delta performers. And then there were the guitars, including one donated by ZZ Top that had incorporated a piece of cypress wood from Muddy's nearby cabin (the cabin itself had recently been bought by the House of Blues and was being shipped to New Orleans), another donated by BB King and an ancient, battered amplified nine-string that Big Joe Williams used most of his life.

As I was driving out of Clarksdale I got a puncture. I phoned round and found the only garage open on Sunday was Morton's, just a mile up the road. When I arrived a few minutes later, a guy in greasy overalls asked, "What took you so long?" I looked at him nonplussed. He pointed to the highway signs hanging over the intersection: 61 and 49. "You can't tour the Delta and leave without visitin' the Crossroads." I felt a chill. I was at *the* crossroads; the crossroads where Robert Johnson, most fabled bluesman of all, had sold his soul to the Devil in exchange for guitar mastery.

NAMSTALGIA

After the rain, the sun

There was no real need to crawl on my belly - the fifty-yard section of the Cu Chi tunnels, 22 miles north-west of Saigon, had been enlarged to take westerners shuffling on their knees. But I wanted to know what it really must have been like to inhabit this hell for months at a time.

I switched off the torch and lay there in the fetid, impenetrable darkness, just as 16,000 Viet Cong had done back in 1966, when B52s were pounding the region. My t-shirt was soaked in sweat, beads ran into my eyes and I tried to close out the sickly smell of rat urine. I quickly switched the torch back on and startled a cockroach.

Returning to the blinding sunlight, I was guided to one of the original unwidened entrances to the 125-mile labyrinthine network. I could only get my legs in. Nearby was the crater a B52 had left and beside it were a number of VC traps (barbed nails and sharpened bamboo stakes in concealed pits). Then it was time for the souvenir picture astride a tank that had been blown up by a VC mine.

The Cu Chi tunnels are the most tangible example of "Namstalgia" - the West's continuing obsession with the first war America lost. There may be 1,001 better reasons for visiting Vietnam as it emerges from the long communist sleep - the idiosyncratic temples, tropical rain forest, 1,400 miles of unspoilt coastline and a French colonial legacy that has bequeathed baguettes and decent coffee to the restaurants - but the images that drew me, and many like me, to Vietnam were burned into our soft, flower-power psyches by The War.

For the visitor, Namstalgia is omnipresent. In Saigon (few locals can bring themselves to call it Ho Chi Minh City) opposite the Good Morning Vietnam bar is the Apocalypse Now Bar and on its wall is a poster for the film *Platoon* with the words: "In War, innocence is the first thing to suffer" (beside it, an airline poster catches the mood with "Vietnam - After the rain, the sun").

They sell the t-shirts, too. And key rings made from empty cartridges. I bought mine along with a dog tag (Salter, Frederick J. US 50203335 A. Positive 574169024. Catholic) and VC badges at the refreshment shack at Cu Chi. I bought a US marine's zip lighter outside the imperial city of the Nguyen kings at Hue. And I bought my Ho Chi Minh t-shirt on the beach at Vung Tau (scene of the final US withdrawal) from Yen Hair, a twenty-year-old from Hanoi, who offered to throw in her body for a further $10.

Namstalgia is clearly marketable and these warm, industrious, pragmatic people are not sentimental. The detritus of the war may look like the real thing, but everything from dog tags to flak jackets is now manufactured in Cholon, Saigon's Chinatown.

The ghost of the war stalks the country. At Phoenix Island in the Mekong Delta is the Disney-esque temple legacy of Nguyễn Thành Nam, also known as the "Coconut Monk". Nguyễn Thành Nam established his syncretic pacifist

Coconut Religion in 1963, was jailed briefly for preaching pacifism and peaceful unification with the north during the war and was then jailed for a good deal longer after the war by the communists.

He died in 1990, by which time his flock had fled, but the gaudy dragons and demons that no doubt tormented him still stand guard in the temple alongside his Apollo rocket launcher made from tin cans.

The equally exotic Cao Dai temple, 54 miles north-west of Saigon, still supports a flock but numbers are dwindling. In the 1950s, the flourishing sect was the centre of the resistance struggle against the French, but in the sixties it was militantly anti-communist. Each day at noon a tide of brilliantly coloured ceremonial gowns float into a temple of eastern baroque - a candy palace where Liberace would have been proud to have been laid to rest. The hour-long hagiolatry, accompanied by haunting music and chants, celebrates a line of saints that includes St John the Baptist, the Prophet Mohammed, Confucius, the Jade Emperor, St Joan and Victor Hugo.

At Marble Mountain, near Danang, three young girls showed me a cave that had served as a VC HQ and another that had been its hospital until a bomb punctured the roof and killed everybody inside (the Buddha miraculously escaped). We ended the tour at Heaven - the name bestowed on the roof of Water Mountain which we reached by scrambling through a narrow fissure in the limestone rock. On the roof of their world, Bai, one of the girls, pointed out China Beach from whose sands I would later dive into the surf just as the GIs had.

In Hué, which endured some of the heaviest fighting, I was told that people still see ghostly images rising from ditches. Having visited the pavilions, gateways and temples, which the bombs had somehow missed in the Imperial City of the Nguyen kings, I cycled through warm rain along the banks of the Perfumed River. Across a dyke, through emerald paddy fields, I watched a boy in a coolie hat seemingly rise out of the ground before slowly pushing his bike away from me.

The war years continue to shape the present in Hué's market. Under a cordillera of conical hats, women sold war souvenirs as a swarm of dragonflies hovered like *huey* helicopters above. It was in this market that I realised the truth of Huysmans' maxim: "The true mark of human genius is artifice". Here was the busyness of the beehive, where, in a frenzy of slapping, rolling, chipping, banging and stretching, a hundred unfathomable objects were being transformed into a thousand further unknowables.

Out on the river, the prows and sterns of the low-slung punts curled up like smiles, many of them built from recycled carcasses of the war. My own eight year-old helmsman had insisted that the aluminium shell of his boat had come from the fuselage of a US plane.

Most of the remains of the war, however, you cannot see; they live in the memories of the people. En route to the Mekong Delta, I met a 69-year-old retired VC who now tends the grounds of a war memorial. Nguyen Ba Tong and his wife had fought and survived the French and Americans before Nguyen's wife was killed by the Khmer Rouge when they poured across the border in 1975.

Outside the old US Embassy in Saigon, I met a 55-year-old who had fought against the VC. As an ex-captain of the 18th Infantry Division he, like countless others, had spent years in a "re-education" camp when the communists took over (during which time his wife and three children died trying to escape by boat to Hong Kong). As another ex-captain from the Vietnamese navy pedalled me through the streets in his cyclo-taxi to the Museum of American War Crimes, he told me of his own incarceration under the communists.

The memories at the museum are equally stark. There are bare statistics on the wall and equally bare propaganda. There are pickled malformed foetuses and appalling photographs of napalm phosphorus and Agent Orange victims. And there are poignant moments - the US medals of Sgt William Brom are displayed against the briefest of notes: "To the People of a United Vietnam. I was wrong. I am sorry. Sgt William Brom, 173 Division."

Increasing numbers of US veterans are returning to the country. On the roof of the Rex Hotel, the old secret CIA HQ, whose exotic roof terrace seems to have taken a leaf out of the Cao Dai architectural excesses, twelve US Vets were swapping memories and sundowners.

Returning GIs gravitate to Saigon because it is the epicentre of Namstalgia where a War Surplus Market (Dan Sinh Market) still sells fatigue green cans of gun oil or fungicidal foot powder, parachutes for $35, hammocks for $4, medals, pennants, gas masks and life belts.

Vietnam, as in the sixties, is on everyone's lips, the latest buzz destination on the tourist map. Hong Kong businessmen, afraid that in 1997 China would attempt to empty their fruit machine, bought insurance with hotels and land purchases along Vietnam's vast unspoilt coastline. The government of the Socialist Republic of Vietnam, meanwhile, eased restrictions on tourist movement in anticipation of the inevitable boom. Then Clinton lifted the trade embargo.

I head out in brilliant sunshine through two-stroke heaven. Along the streets people cobble, sell drinks, heat up soup, fix car tyres and sell lottery tickets or baguettes in front of flaking colonial buildings. Cyclos cruise alongside the pavement offering, "I take you best places… Where you going? I take you." And Vietnam has so many great places to take even the most jaded tourist. Some complain that that our presence is sending prices through the bamboo roof, but for the West it remains an absurdly cheap destination.

Until the coach juggernauts and cruise liners arrive, and they will, the experience is poignant and pregnant with possibility. The Vietnamese have mourned and moved on; they realise there is more to life than death. Everywhere you go you feel the irrepressible energy. The people smile and laugh a lot more than we do. They do not seem to harbour grudges nor are they preoccupied by war although they're not averse to turning a buck from those who are. The Vietnam War may have been one of the most shameful moments in America's history, but for Vietnam it was a short war following on the heels of resistance struggles against the French, Japanese and Chinese (the latter lasted 1,000 years, the American War just ten).

In Vietnam you can buy any number of souvenirs, but my own favourite - epitomising the pragmatism, artistry and industry of the people - are the replica *huey* helicopters made from local beer and soft drink cans. I have one hanging in the hall at home.

ONLY IN JAPAN

Through the looking glass

ALASKAN LONELY HEARTS CLUB

The American occupation of Japan may have technically ended in 1952 but to all intents and purposes it still continues. Nam veterans who preferred the prospect of obedient Japanese brides to feisty American ones teach English instead of collecting welfare support; legions of US businessmen attempt to even up the trade gap; and bullet-headed ex-marines work the nightclubs. In Japan you'll find baseball diamonds, black greased quiffs and silicon valleys. But although a large slice of the country, like the rest of the world, is American, visitors to the Land of Rising Sun will soon enough be rubbing their eyes, mumbling like Dorothy, "Toto, I don't think we're in Kansas anymore."

Arriving at Tokyo's Narita airport after touring the chaos and vibrancy of other Asian countries one is initially seduced by the surface resemblance. Colours are European monochrome, everything works, the subway's clean and shops are full of goods similar to those back home. Differences in Japan are more to do with mindscape rather than landscape; disparities are small but cavernous.

At the karaoke club in Shinjuku's Niagara of light, deep-fried chrysanthemums and lilies are being served. In the Seibu department store someone is bowing on the end of a telephone. Out on the streets pedestrian crossings play "Coming through the Rye", directional signs are in braille and office workers move quickly like at home but wear surgical masks across their mouths. Outside banks there are ceremonial cabbage beds rather than flower baskets; inside the banks there are pornographic magazines for queueing customers to flick through.

Sooner or later every visitor comes to the realisation that Japan is both weird and culturally as far from the West as it is geographically. The Japanese may wear suits like those back home, but what inhabits them is pure otherness. In 1970, before the consumer frenzy really bit, Tokyoites already had 1.4 TVs per person fitting into 25 square feet of personal living space (65 square feet is generally accepted the minimum required before society starts to disintegrate). Then the city, with one of the densest population concentrations in the world, took up golf for a hobby.

In the teeming capital the pachinko parlour is the psychotic centre: the exteriors a galaxy of sprinting neon, the interiors a cacophony of crashing silver balls. Fourteen million Japanese may find vertical pinball irresistible, but as gambling is forbidden, winners must collect a "prize" rather than money then head round the back of the building where they exchange it for cash.

The Japanese are ruled not by the moral kernel of their laws but by the imperative to be seen to be obeying. Integrity in Japan concerns itself with the surface - you are what you appear (our nearest approximation is probably "manners maketh man"). Foreigners mistakenly accuse the Japanese of hypocrisy. But this is simplistic; they just use a different cultural cement. Japan has seen too many earthquakes not to take notice of cracks. The surface is what holds society together.

Amusement arcades are less popular than pachinko parlours but invariably full. One of the favourite games here involves the player using a mallet to hammer down an army of projectiles that appear above an undulating table. In Japan if something sticks up, you hammer it down.

Japanese pornography laws show a similar concern with the surface. On suburban street corners alongside beer dispensers (Kirin - "Drink Up Enjoy Refreshing Time") and condom machines ("Play Safe with Wrinkle Chapeau Condom") I discovered explicit porn mags dispensers which brazenly display rape or bestiality with impunity but eschew showing a single female pubic hair for fear of prosecution.

Even the young, who profess to be in open revolt against the boa constrictor of Japanese society, restrict their rebellion to the cosmetic. At Tokyo's Yoyogi Park I watched teenage girls balance on their wooden sandals as they slipped out of their kimonos into a pot-pourri of the last half century's pop styles - rockabilly, glam, punk, rave, Goth and grunge. Sundays at Yoyogi is a celebration of rebel youth culture without the rebellion. The hurricane of styles is worn with no social context: no mods and rockers dust-ups on the beach, no rock 'n roll at the barricades, no punk anarchy - just the gear. Young girls on all fours whipping the pavement with their long silky hair in devotion to their favourite band is about as violent as it gets. Others dance manically in sixty-second bursts to a battery of ghetto blasters pumping out anything from Eddie Cochrane to Metallica and then stop and resume their pouting and grooming.

When they are done with mincing for the cameras, they slip back into the kimonos and head across the park to the Meiji shrine to put a coin in a box and make a wish. More likely than not they'll also purchase a good luck charm against traffic accidents for their father, another for their mother's good health and a third for success in their own forthcoming exams. And they'll all be home before nightfall.

The fact that each year 3.5 million people visit Japan and 13.5 million leave or holiday abroad speaks volumes of the Japanese need for escape. But it would be a big mistake to confuse this with a lack of respect for their culture.

A couple of streets from the bedlam of Ueno Station, I found a salaryman practising his golf swing off a rubber car mat in an alley beside small wooden homes whose balconies were festooned with geraniums and bonsais.

The greatest cultural achievement of the Japanese has been the refined aesthetic sense that can create an oasis out of the smallest possible space. Tokyo has more than 7,000 parks, many of them the size of a handkerchief, but in each you'll find a couple of ornamental trees and maybe a carp pond. They may come sushi-sized but they'll always squeeze in a scattering of stone lanterns and a couple of Buddhas.

Once the thirteen metro lines and street signs (or lack of them) are negotiated, Tokyo opens like a lotus flower to museums devoted exclusively to kites, salt and yes, flowers.

The city is also paradoxically slavishly devoted to bigness - from the world's largest fish market (Tsukiji) to Electric City, a suburb inhabited solely by electrical department stores - but this is precisely why the inhabitants deify the small and delicate from bonsai to origami. No city has higher buildings nor shorter skirts.

Scouring the upcoming events column in *Tokyo Cityscope*, the monthly listings mag, I found a bullfinch exchange festival, an exhibition of flower paintings and a parade for a long-dead haiku poet. The Japanese go their own way. Literally. Between 1988 and 1993 public bowing reputedly nudged 24 passers-by to their deaths on escalators, trains and revolving doors. Like sumo, which elevates wrestling from sham to high aesthetic, it may be as weird as hell but it's compulsive and compelling.

Stepping into a small yakatori in the more traditional downtown district of Nezu with the owner of the ryokan I was staying at, I discovered the essence of this aesthetic. I was now as far from Shinjuku's flickering video screens and forty-storey Roman Candles as it was possible to get. Steam swirled from the soup in the metal oden and chicken sizzled on the grill as a bald-headed chef and Mrs Suzuki, the yakatori owner, sang along to a tremulous crooner on the TV. A plumber, who always popped in for a second dinner after an earlier one at home (he hated his wife's cooking but couldn't bring himself to tell her), chatted with a subway driver at the bar who in turn lassoed us into the conversation.

After beer and sake, my host Mr Sawa, ordered us pints of shochu (Japanese vodka) with oolong tea. At the bottom of the glass I discovered a plum. Like the world's cultured pearls that were first produced by Mikimoto Kokichi and sold in Tokyo over a century ago, the city conceals its greatest charms. After endless dishes ranging from small fish fried and eaten whole to grilled chicken with gingko nuts, eggplant, sesame and miso, the bill for four came to £50.

Down the alleyways that led back to the ryokan, the wooden two-storey homes were covered with heavy, curling stone tiles (*kawara*) and the balconies occupied by bonsai gardens and old boneshaker bicycles. As we walked and Mr Sawa's traditional blue worker's outfit flapped above his clacking wooden sandals like bird's wings, he pointed out the kimono mender's workshop and the studio of a local watercolour artist. Both, he claimed, had been there thirty years.

Back at our base, Mr Sawa took out his seventeen-year-old cockatoo for a chat while I retired to one of two steaming public baths. I had it to myself and meditated on a picture of snow-covered Mount Fuji, left there exactly for that purpose. I then retired to my futon on the tatami, watched the sumo basho being broadcast from Kyushu, Japan's westernmost island where I'd once spent three months teaching English. I sipped more oolong tea and drifted off to sleep dreaming of vast slabs of tuna wrestling in a sumo *doyo* watched over by a sage-like Mount Fuji.

PASS THE BRAIN TABLETS

Healing and dowsing in Basingstoke

O n the "Health" shelves were *The Healing Power of Pollen*, *Fears, Phobias and Panic*, *Moxibustion* (the therapeutic application of heat to acupuncture points) and even *Vaginismus* (involuntary spasms preventing intercourse) but absolutely nothing on Healing and Dowsing. I turned back to my Weekend Break Information Sheet for clues. Under the "What to Bring" section I found one: "If you don't have your own pendulum, it is easy to make one quickly and cheaply. A heavy ring, metal nut or washer will do, on a length of stout twine approximately 8" long." I raided my tool box, came up with a heavy nut, found a rather grotty bit of string and joined them. I hoped my pendulum would not embarrass me in what I fully anticipated would be a roomful of glistening designer crystals.

Our healing and dowsing weekend was devised and hosted by Jack Temple whose contribution to the information sheet was succinct and oracular. "People have been turning in ever greater numbers to dowsing with a pendulum for their greater protection." The choice of venue was equally inspired.

Basingstoke was enigmatic: a towering Blade Runner city re-christened BM. Tarmac streams wove past tight-lipped glass monsters to the outskirts of town where anonymous lodges and bungalows slept through afternoon kips on manicured lawns. At the creepily impersonal Hilton Lodge someone was checking in at reception ahead of me with a healing and dowsing weekend voucher. I breathed a sigh of relief that I wouldn't be alone.

At the 7pm welcome reception, pendulums were already out and swinging. I pushed my nut further into a cavern in my pocket and struck up a conversation with Richard from Southsea who graphically talked me through Jack Temple's miraculous cure of a nasty throat problem he'd had the previous year. Richard positively beamed with evangelical health and vitality as did his wife and daughter, though in the latter's case I was less convinced she was in possession of a full complement of nuts and washers.

After dinner, sixty experienced and virgin dowsers filed into the Winchester Room for our general introduction. Jack's aim for the weekend was "To open your minds to self-help." A noble aim. "Last time at Huddersfield we concentrated on prostates and periods; this time we'll look at spines." One woman exclaimed shirtily, "Excuse me, I did not come here to learn about periods." The rest of us free-thinkers laughed expansively. I looked around. Slightly more than half the audience appeared to be over fifty. Jack himself, a halo of electric white hair (or was it aura?) and oozing good health, was in his seventies. Amazingly, he told us, just eight weeks earlier he'd lost three stone and nearly died following a nasty bout of coral poisoning in Mauritius. Realising he was slipping away, he discharged himself from hospital, "closed my sphincter muscles" and "been right as rain ever since".

Dowsing, we learnt, was an ancient art and there were many different types of dowsers. The best-known of these were those who divined water but there were others who map dowsed, distance dowsed and witness dowsed. Tomorrow we would learn about miasmic magnetic distortions from ancestors and be taught to "vacuum our systems". I could hardly wait.

Jack was already in full swing when I made a belated entrance the next morning: "...first of all today we're going to remove the toxic debris from our brains". Jack walked the aisles pointing his middle finger at us and mumbling to his pendulum. Three males were identified as having lead in the brain (assorted debris contributors included vaccinations, toothpaste, dental fillings, sanitary towels, nappies, hair dye and make up). I, naturally, was one of them. A frantic one-sided conversation between Jack and his pendulum followed. "Is the brain operating ten out of ten?" … vigorous anticlockwise swinging … "nine out of ten?" … nope. "Eight, seven, six, five, four, three?" The pendulum lay doggo. I was devastated. A three-out-of-ten operative power in the right hemisphere? And I've always felt that was my better side. Jack deliberated and finally decided on a course of treatment and a number of tablets were duly taped to my scalp (the body is porous and treatment is apparently by osmosis).

Soon the room resembled a battlefield with the war wounded wandering with tablet trails running down their faces, marching over the rims of ears, across heads and down feet.

A little later it was my turn again. This time it was my back (I've suffered lower back pains for over a year now). Jack ran his finger down the vertebrae until the pendulum located the problem - a miasm inherited from my great, great grandfather as a result of his scarlet fever. "The miasm has prevented you from absorbing nat sulph."

"Nat sulph?"

"Nat sulph." Jack strapped more tablets to me before we hurried through the rest of the world's great diseases. My own collection included osteoporosis over the right eye (inflamed) and the right thumb (apparently causing left-sided chest pains). In short I had strains of scarlet fever in my spine, crumbling bones and a brain that was an embarrassment.

This was not my idea of a weekend break but I drew comfort from the fate of others. My immediate neighbour had pill lines across the head, cheekbones and ears and was still awaiting the start of a saliva flow to cure her indigestion (jaundice on her mother's side 900 years ago). Peggy from Pinner was eagerly strapping more tablets to her ears and swinging her pendulum like a priest with a censer. Despite the fact that she only attended her first dowsing six months earlier, she had usurped both Barbara's pole position as official assistant and nudged ahead of several other experienced healers and dowsers.

Meanwhile my own pendulum refused to budge. I gave it a swing with my right hand and waited for it to choose a direction. I simultaneously applied the middle finger of my left hand to the left side of my neighbour's nostril and asked the pendulum about the state of his liver. The pendulum turned clockwise. Yes, he had a liver. Was it a good liver? The pendulum swung anti-clockwise. I'd guessed as much and shook my head portentously. Then Jack went and spoiled it by noticing Dan had his legs crossed (crossed wires). Checking Dan himself, he gave his liver a ten out of ten.

Notwithstanding this setback, as we neared lunch I was twirling my washer like a string of worry beads, which of course in a way it was.

After lunch we practised "witness dowsing" which involved dowsing blood, hair or spit. Jack's pendulum decided we should go for spit and selected Elaine to provide the specimen. In this morsel, Jack informed us, was the whole Elaine. Through her "witness" we could check all her organs. We dutifully marched past spinning our pendulums and diagnosing every galactic illness that had struck or missed our planet. The spittle was a very sick spittle.

To a healing and dowsing neophyte, his or her pendulum is his or her doctor, guru and Holy Ghost. I already knew there were water dowsers, map dowsers, distance dowsers and witness dowsers but on the second morning I learned there were also credit card dowsers.

Peggy, our geopathic witness and gall bladder dowser, plumped herself down at my table, grabbed my free hand and told me I had come to her in a dream the night before. Apparently my name was Rowan and I was 400 years old and I had come seeking help with a bloated bubonic neck. I smiled, thanked her for whatever help she had given me and attempted to switch tables. But Peggy was made of Teflon. She grabbed my arm, pulled me back down, whirled her pendulum in a frenzy round my watch and thrust her middle finger through the vortex to neutralise the negative energy. "You've got to watch credit cards too. Give me your credit cards to neutralise."

I looked around the restaurant. Other dowsing colleagues were dangling pendulums over the buffet spread, checking the dynamic force of the baked Alaskas and salami. Others sat at tables running their fingers down the menu as if reading braille before seeking their pendulums' recommendations. Someone enthusiastically announced from another table, "We got a gall bladder here, one out of ten." I raised an eyebrow in feigned admiration as Pam called across to Peggy, "Noticeable difference in saliva flow." But Peggy was not to be distracted. "Give me your credit cards and check your house for geopathic rays when you get home."

I looked round the restaurant once more and noticed that other non-dowsing weekend breakers were avoiding all eye contact with us. We were a leper colony in the Basingstoke Hilton Lodge. I gathered up my cleared credit cards and headed for the Winchester Room for our final session where we were to practise more food dowsing to protect us from supermarkets.

First we checked a lettuce and it passed with flying colours, but when a bottle of orange squash came out a chorus of "Ooooohs" went up as if a battalion of Nazi stormtroopers had just burst in. Fingers pointed and pendulums swung in the dowsing equivalent of brandishing the crucifix at vampires. We ooohed some more at its irredeemable wickedness and then moved on to kitchen utensils. Jack told us that apart from taking out a second mortgage to have our fillings removed, the next best thing we could do for our families was to throw out our aluminium saucepans. Another neophyte in the audience confided, "I'm worried about non-stick pans too." "So am I," Jack confessed.

I started to feel hugely grumpy. Maybe I was suffering geopathic stress from the air conditioning. At our last supper I went wild and ate my broccoli without seeking my pendulum's permission. I left with thirty tablets strapped to my back (my great great grandfather's scarlet fever) and a complimentary bottle of brain tablets (BC-6 cocoa butter and maturite made from a meoterite found in Malaysia). I have taken my first BC-6 but do not expect to be filling in a MENSA membership form quite yet.

Q-Tips and Breath Tablets

Asian scams

Travellers' scams aim either to make money or avoid spending it. They can range from bunking into a hotel swimming pools to carrying gold into Kathmandu. For the impecunious a good scam can be the difference between three months more on a Goan beach or a hasty return to the dole queue back home.

Just as there's kudos for those travellers who manage to live on half a shoe-string, similarly those that pull off the biggest scams soon go down in travellers' folklore. One case I heard of in three different Asian cities was of a Sheffield man who'd lost a finger in an industrial accident at home and subsequently claimed for it on five separate holiday insurances.

So many travellers make bogus claims that legitimate claims, such as the one I made for a theft on the Bombay-Goa steamer, are rejected. American Express is similarly suspicious of traveller cheque losses. The scam here is selling originals at one-third face value before claiming for replacement cheques. In Hong Kong I saw an elderly American tourist undergo a grilling that would have had an SAS man spilling the beans.

For those who prefer prison in Kathmandu to the dole queue there's the lucrative gold run. This not only takes nerve but also superb sphincter muscle control carrying 1kg of gold up the rear end. For me a free air ticket and $600 cash would not compensate for a chronic spastic colon.

Less risky is the three-day smuggling trip to Taiwan, Tokyo and sometimes South Korea which Dave, a Canadian ex-air steward I trekked with in Nepal, organises from Hong Kong, paying $200 plus food, lodging and air tickets. Harry, at the travellers' guesthouse in Chung-King mansions, runs similar trips for $100 carrying clothes, gadgets and cameras past a paid-off Taipei customs man. Cartier imitation watches are then taken to Tokyo before the traveller is flown back to Hong Kong.

DIY smuggling is even more popular. The illegal exchange of cash dollars on the black market and the 100 per cent profit made in just about every Asian city on duty-free booze and cigarettes (Johnny Walker Red Label and 555 State Express are usually preferred) are just the tip of the iceberg. As long as you don't mind local currency, or better, are willing to exchange for local goods, then a profit can easily be made on the cheaper calculators, videos and electrical equipment. Then there's the big league... Selling passports is very risky, drug smuggling suicide. Buying gems in Thailand (exchanged by Burmese guerrillas on the Thai border for weapons) demands great care and knowledge. A Toxteth couple we met made $8,000 in Nepal on an eight-year-old Mercedes diesel van and spare parts. This is obviously a lucrative trade but takes a lot of work, large initial outlay and is fraught with red tape and pay offs. Buying large quantities of saris in Varanasi to sell in Bangladesh needs the right contracts plus luck at the customs or more greasing of palms. Personally I'd rather take breath tablets and bananas into Korea.

Indeed, it was sailing to South Korea on the Shimonoseki-Pusan overnight ferry from Honshu (Japan) that I met scam travelling in its purest form. The departure lounge was full of overweight middle-aged women with enormous bundles of clothes, jars of coffee and crates of bananas. A blonde American Born-Again from Redneck country enquired if I was married then moved straight into the "Y'all like ta do me a BIIGG faver an' take these here li'l crates erv ban a nas through them Ko ree een custerms fowa me?"

Five minutes later, a westerner resembling Eraserhead struck a deal with us to carry his excess duty frees. His passport was a work of art: pages ripped out, others sewn in, numbers changed, drink stains obscuring unwanted entries or exits. He was just returning from three months in a Japanese detention centre for selling $1,000-worth of travellers' cheques and was travelling in the most expensive cabin but had paid only tatami class. Scamming had been his life since he left Brighton twenty years earlier and everybody on board, including the crew, knew him.

I passed through customs successfully with Redneck Jesus, Eraserhead, an Israeli draft dodger, a Nigerian from Alabama, a Filipino, an Iranian and a Minnesota track star. They were all smuggling and/or working illegally in Japan and crossing for visas.

Burma, as a country, is Asia's number one scamming destination. At the airport's state bank exchange I was asked if I wanted money "Above the counter" or "Out the pocket". The cashier then offered to buy my duty frees. Upstairs a waiter informed me that no beer was available but he would be willing to sell us his own at $2 a bottle. We exchanged $5 officially then went to Rangoon's Diplomatic Store to buy another batch of duty frees before selling the whole lot (800 cigarettes and four bottles of whisky) for a fifty per cent profit. We also exchanged a ghetto blaster I found on the streets of Tokyo for about $70 worth of laquerwork.

On departure, anomalies on the official form (where all transactions should have been recorded) are overlooked if the customs officer finds a dollar tucked into your passport. Even the seven-day-stay restriction can be got around by losing your Biman air ticket the day before departure as it takes two days to be replaced and flights are only once a week.

Talking of Biman, apart from usually being the cheapest available, the Bangladeshi airline (fondly known as Banglacrash - "It's late or belated") is popular because its non-flights often involve enforced stopovers on full board. In Dacca we managed to crash six friends on full board on our tickets.

While travelling for a year in Asia, apart from the welcome weight losses, I sometimes felt my social skills similarly shrinking on a conversational diet of bowel movements and travellers' scams. Small scams which don't involve ripping off individuals can be a fun part of travelling. But obsessional scammers, who only see countries in terms of angles, seem to me to be into a similar ball game as the devoted city businessman. Both cultivate ulcers in the name of Mammon and with over three million other deities in India alone to be considered, why pick this one?

RAIL ALE TRAIL

The Oblivion Express

My friend Ken slowly but surely wore down my resistance. "These are th peerless buffet bars of God's own country the like of which you'll neve find anywhere else in the world." There was a momentary pause while Ken waited in vain for a response. "You do realise CAMRA tickers come from all ove to visit the West Riding buffet bars? It's probably the most important stretch o railway track in the whole of Europe."

Ken made his monthly pub crawl of a Yorkshire railway spur sound hal Lourdes pilgrimage, half cultural tour on the Trans-Siberian Railway. The hallowed buffet bars - The Riverhead Tap, The Head of Steam and The Sayer - were Ken' *stations* of the cross. Incidentally, "rail tickers" are a recent mutation of the rai anorak, who instead of collecting train numbers tick off real ales they've supped a buffet bars before cataloguing and indexing them. Ken wished to distance himsel from his CAMRA brethren. "Our group of railway explorers are not of their cloth We don't drink halves and then move on. The Lord didn't make half days so why have half pints? If we like a pint somewhere, we may stay several days."

Ken's printed itinerary for his "Rail Ale Trail" outing from Stalybridge in Greater Manchester to Dewsbury in Yorkshire and back was suitably oracula when it duly arrived. The pilgrims numbered eight and included Mike "CAMRA" Robinson, Aussie Bob, Phil the Farrars, Pete the Print and Mundc Hicks. According to our instructions, our liquid odyssey would start early "10am assemble for quick coffee at the White Hart at Lydgate. 10.30am leave for Stalybridge Buffet Bar with hamper, pies, drinks and disposable glasses."

It was at our initial rendezvous that things immediately went awry in a manner that suggested it was more habit than one off. The "quick coffee" turned into two pints of Windy Miller - and in some cases three ("Breakfast," according to Phil Garratt, wine merchant owner of Vins de Bordeaux in Oldham and our group leader). We consequently would miss our first train but no one seemed unduly concerned. "It's probably late anyway," Phil the Print noted. Waiting for the next train just meant we'd have longer at our first real place of pilgrimage, the Stalybridge Buffet Bar.

In the hagiology of British pubs, the Stalybridge Buffet Bar must nestle at the top, or very near to it, and is today much like it probably was when it opened for business in 1885: blink and you can imagine troops from nearby Ladysmith Barracks nipping in for a pint before heading off to India or the trenches. Outside, a windswept platform gave way to vistas of denuded Pennine hills. Inside, Tommy Chandwick - a dapper former marine and retired ambulanceman with handlebar moustache - was putting more coal on the fire and simultaneously announcing that the 12.46 to York would be fifteen minutes late. On the walls were advertisements for Lyons Tea and Capstan cigarettes. A dispenser offered platform tickets for 1d, fairy lights chased each other round indows, tulip lamps sprouted from overhead paddle fans, and a line of buffed and pumps gleamed invitingly from behind the bar. The list of this week's pecials was displayed like a hymn sheet: Bitter Sweet Memory from Shropshire, Crackle from Barnsley... We ordered eight pints of the former (£1.90 a pint) and en bowls of the speciality black peas in salt and vinegar (50p).

All too soon the tardy Trans-Pennine Express to York pulled in and we nuddled aboard. Once seated Phil Garratt - instigator of the tour and its archivist launched into his evangelical confirmation classes for the new boy, enlightening ne on the comparative merits of towns and their pubs (coincidentally the best owns all seemed to have the best bars). The "rail ale pubs" were the punctuation narks in Phil Garratt's sermon on the Pennines.

As we romped on our iron horse across "the land of mist and mutton", taggeringly beautiful Pennine countryside gave way to equally sublime esurrected wool towns. Although the rail journey out to Dewsbury (our furthest oint) and back would only take around ninety minutes total travelling time, it vould be twelve hours before we returned to the White Hart.

Once into the journey, Aussie Bob (so named not because he is Australian ut because he imports Australian wines) delved into our accompanying hamper. A bottle of Pol Roger was duly popped and a toast made to a fruitful day just as ve entered the 3.5-mile long Standedge Tunnel. Charles Brierley, owner of the White Hart, handed round the bacon sandwiches, and Aussie Bob immediately aunched into his spiel. "A fine choice of provision if I may say so Charles. As or the Pol Roger, it's clean … it's fresh … its beautifully rising mousse mixing pectacularly with the saltiness of the butty."

"Pol Roger was Churchill's favourite," historian Phil chipped in, "and is first parliamentary seat was of course Oldham, where my own wine shop appens to be located." It was then time for ex-professional rugby league player Mundo to raise the scatological stakes. "It's a little known fact that Churchill was he last white man in Britain to be called Winston. I share a birthday with him .. and Frank Ifield - November 30th. My dad wanted to call me Winston but lecided on Raymond instead."

There was a momentary, reverential silence as we passed the millstone grit mphitheatre of Marsden with its wrap-round 5,000-acre moorland tended by he National Trust. At Huddersfield we disembarked to change trains. "Three ninutes before the Dewsbury departure. Time for a pint," Phil announced before leading us into The Head of Steam on Platform One.

As Phil and the boys got the first round in, Mundo took me outside to admire the station façade. The buffet bar exit into the town is through Corinthian columns that are a miniature of the grand pedimented entranceway to the station itself. Mundo pointed to the George Hotel opposite: "That's where rugby league was first established when local teams broke off from the South." Mundo knew about such things having played semi-pro with Oldham and Keighley for fifteen years. With his three-quarter leather and fur trimmed coat, black trousers, splayed feet and athletic rolling walk, he could have starred in any cult gangster film of the past thirty years.

Amazingly we managed to drag Phil and the rest of the gang back onto the platform to catch the Dewsbury train in a little under an hour. At our terminus we headed straight for the buffet bar - this one more respectfully known as The West Riding Licensed Refreshment Rooms. A coal fire was burning in a corner and a juke box playing the Red Hot Chili Peppers' "Californication". There didn't seem much of that in Yorkshire - Californication I mean. A sturdy punctilious clock stood on a wall above bilious green wainscoting. Meanwhile lace curtains in the chapel-like windows concealed the town's vulgar commerce from the bar's parishioners. On tap was Twister from the local Ossett Brewery, Slaters from Staffordshire, Salamander from Bradford and an Anglo-Dutch beer brewed in Dewsbury itself. Mundo was by now sleeping blissfully in front of a half empty pint glass (he has been known to fall into the deepest slumber even on bar stools). The owner of The West Riding Licensed Refreshment Rooms, Mike Field, smiled: "Another satisfied customer."

It was Mike, I would later be told, along with Phil Holdsworth of the Riverhead Brewery in Marsden, Tony Brookes (Head of Steam) and John Hesketh (Stalybridge Buffet Bar) who dreamed up the local Rail Ale Trail toward the tail of the last millennium. And Mike today remains as passionate about the rail route from Stalybridge to Dewsbury as he was when he was merely a fan rather than a publican (he rescued the bar a decade ago after a sixty-year hiatus in its career). "This stretch is the cream, if you'll excuse the pun, of the northern real ale rail trail, and part of its appeal - apart of course from our peerless buffet bars which you won't find anywhere else - is that less time is needed on the train between outstanding watering holes."

Back on the platform, a long yellow hornet buzzed towards us and came to a shuddering halt. We hurtled - or more accurately waddled - towards it beneath a cat's cradle of iron girders supporting an opaque glass canopy through which blinding light attacked our mole eyes. Once more aboard the Oblivion Express, Aussie Bob opened bottles of Cockfighter's Ghost Shiraz 2000. Plastic glasses were dispensed to fellow passengers as our private party was extended to the entire carriage. Bob again got into a canter: "Note the hint of slightly spicy wild blackberries." Passengers, lubricated by the unexpected elixir, chatted freely as snippets of lives were exchanged as quickly as the scenery - buxom hills with rouge lipsticked clouds giving way to crocketed church spires peering over skeletal trees and slumbering towns.

Once again at Huddersfield we had to change trains and inevitably Phil led us into a buffet bar, this time to The Huddersfield Station Tavern, twin sister of The Head of Steam further up the same platform. Like its sister, the Tavern enjoys a good live jazz evening occasionally but in the glare of daylight its stage looked rather forlorn. We only stopped for the one before boarding the Stalybridge bound train where Aussie Bob this time handed round Uncle Joe's Mint Balls - "A dusky minty glacial tang with a hint of eucalyptus." With few vacant seats, our gregarious party had willingly scattered, linking with new captive partners in their attempt to spread blessings and the communion cup.

By now daylight had turned to dusk and was rushing for darkness. We disembarked at Marsden - one of the most photogenic of Yorkshire moorland towns - crossed a bridge over the parallel Huddersfield Narrow Canal and walked 200 yards (the furthest distance we walked all day) beneath the silhouetted Pennines. Eventually at the silver-tongued confluence of two disputatious streams of the River Colne, to peeling church bells, we entered the Riverhead Brewery.

In a corner of the open-plan bar, a glass window looked onto the on-site microbrewery where moorland reservoir water was magically transformed into ale. The beers on tap at the Riverhead have been named after the reservoirs from whence they came: the higher the reservoir, the stronger the alcoholic content. They ranged from a dark mild to a black liquoricey stout, with four bitters of differing strengths in between. The owner, Phil Holdsworth, chatted to the boys, informing them he was planning a real ale cruise along the river to celebrate his sixtieth birthday in a few months' time. When I commended him on his youthful looks he replied, "If I'd drunk Carling instead of real ale I'd probably look eighty. Brewing is like cooking - look after the ingredients and the ingredients look after you."

In fact there is no cooking at the Riverhead ... no music either ... nor slot machines nor karaoke ... just the contented babble of conversation. When Phil converted the former grocer's a decade earlier, Marsden's population of 5,000 already had 23 pubs and clubs vying for its wages. The Riverhead has never looked back.

Eventually, somewhat miraculously, twelve hours after our departure, we managed to find our way back to the White Hart where we all continued to sing from the same hymn sheet, ordering scallops on black pudding for starters followed by sirloin steak. The meal was as successful as the bottles of claret Charles ordered to accompany it. "Is there a finer marriage on earth than full-bloodied beef to a full bodied claret?" Aussie Bob asked. There was not the slightest murmur of dissent.

SKIING IN STRANGE PLACES

Taking the piste in Algeria, Cyprus, Japan and Alaska

Some people learn to ski on dry ski slopes, others on Alpine nursery slopes but as far as I know, I'm the only person who's ever been taught by a drunken French science teacher in a pine forest in Algeria. It explains a lot about my technique.

In the mid-1980s, newly qualified, I took up an appointment as an English teacher in a lycée in Draa El Mizan, a small town in the Djudjura foothills southeast of Algiers. One evening early in my stay, I arrived at a French colleague's apartment for dinner. I knocked on the door, ready to declare every delicacy *formidable*. Jean-Yves, however, did not invite me in. Instead he thrust a sack into my hands, slammed the door behind him and scampered down the stairs with an "On y va". Apparently we were off to catch dinner.

Ten minutes later, approaching a partially dry river bed, I heard a litany of curses … *merde* … *putain* … as five of our teacher friends exploded in frustration at every unsuccessful attempt to grab a frog. Sometimes the expletives were louder and bluer as they slipped in the mud and fouled their clothes. There were, however, the occasional successes and soon my friends' sacks were throbbing with amphibian life while mine remained resolutely lifeless.

After 45 minutes Alain announced it was time to return to Jean-Yves' flat. As the latter served us large celebratory glasses of Pernod, Patrick took the sacks onto the balcony where he started attacking them with a rolling pin. By the time the frogs had been skinned, dowsed in garlic and cooked, it was past midnight.

The dinner, inevitably, turned into a bit of a session and at 4.30am someone suddenly suggested that as it was Saturday we should try Tikjda. By now I was game for pretty much anything even though I had no idea what Tikjda was. A boardgame perhaps?

By the time our headlights started raking the Djudjura pine forest, dawn was already creeping up the mountain. For a couple of hours we dozed in cars until we were woken by machinery cranking up our hangovers. I painfully half opened my eyes and discovered we were parked in a small resort next to a ski lift.

Half an hour later I was booted and suited (fortunately, or unfortunately as it turned out, someone had brought a spare ski jacket and trousers for me). Gérard then informed me that because he had once been a ski instructor he had been designated my handler. First he showed me how to put on my skis, second he demonstrated the snow plough position, which I found slightly obscene, and then without further ado he hooked me to the first available drag lift up the mountain.

Having unravelled me from the fencing at the other end, Gérard led off down the precipitous mountain. I did my best but there were too many trees. Following my visit, Tikjda probably needed a re-forestation programme. My first skiing experience ended with me suspended in a net beside the mid-station lift which, for some reason, my French colleagues found hysterically funny before they abandoned me and continued merrily on their way. It took thirty minutes for the lift attendant and a passing Good Samaritan to unravel me and help me down the slope.

Several years later I was again teaching overseas but this time in Kitakyushu, a kind of Japanese Sheffield, which also happened at the time to be the world's biggest steel town. On this occasion it was a Japanese friend, Kikutchi, who suggested a ski trip several hours' drive away at a resort in the Hiroshima prefecture. We left at 3am and arrived at the slopes just as they were opening. Gayhoku did not even warrant a mention in the Japanese Tourist Organization's list of its top 20 ski resorts and yet the place was heaving.

My friend naturally had his own equipment. I didn't. Instead I spent the next two hours trailing around every ski hire shop in the resort trying to find size ten boots. "Kitsui sugimas" - "They're too small" - I complained. "Yes," the assistant invariably replied with a smile. They had nothing bigger than an eight. In the end, desperate for the slopes, I took the size eight and quickly found out what it must have been like to be a Chinese girl growing up with bound feet. To make matters worse, the queues to the lifts were ridiculously long. Over the next four hours I managed a grand total of twenty minutes' actual skiing.

My next overseas teaching assignment was to the sun-drenched island of Cyprus where I was pleasantly surprised to discover that this was a place where you really could ski on snow in the morning and on water in the afternoon. I lived in Cyprus for four years and couldn't wait for winter. At weekends I'd strap my skis (I had a pair of my own by then) along the saddle of my motorbike so they extended a couple of feet beyond the rear rack. I'd then pop my boots into a rucksack and point the bike towards the Troodos Mountains.

It would take the best part of two hours to reach Mount Olympus and it became particularly dicey when I reached the snow line and had to negotiate compacted snow or ice on two wheels. It was, however, always worth it. Often I overnighted in the ski club's mixed-sex lodge where I was invariably the only person over sixteen and my companions, having slipped their parents' leashes, were clearly intent on making the most of it. The lodge was very cheap but the price didn't include sleep. Instead, as I listened to adolescent fumblings, I stared into the roaring log fire that glowed through the night and quietly pondered why there had been no ski lodges when I was a schoolboy growing up in Liverpool.

Cyprus is a very long way from Alaska where I ended up a decade later. At the goldmining town of Girdwood, the resort of Alyeska had grown up hopeful that skiing would be the new goldmine. A-frame cabins wore two-foot snow moustaches and dagger icicles dangled from overhangs like earrings.

On the breakfast menu at the Alyeska Bake Shop cinnamon rolls instead of reindeer sausage was the giveaway that this was a granola resort aimed at alternative types rather than frontier Neanderthals; a place where local women shun make up and teach meditation while their husbands work as masseurs rather than as lumberjacks and gold miners.

Alyeska claims to be the lowest ski resort (250 feet) in the US, and as such there's no enduring two-hour corkscrew drives to reach it and no panting for breath when skiing. Yet it still manages to regularly figure in the top four for snow coverage and, according to *Condé Nast Traveller*, has the best views of any US ski area - from the Glacier Terminal there's a clear sweep across the Chugach Mountains, Turnagain Arm and seven hanging glaciers.

Apart from regular downhill, telemark and cross-country, Alyeska provides a smorgasbord of other activities from *skijoring* to mushing and snowmobiling. So, having spent a day swooping down eerily empty slopes, I exchanged my skis for snow shoes and set off to explore more wilderness. The bears, I'd been assured, were all hibernating. But, being a sceptic by nature, I nervously fingered the just-in-case pepper spray I had in my pocket each time another slab of snow crashed from a tree and scared me half to death. My greatest fear was that I might wake one of the black bears fond of the spicy Cajun diet provided by the dumper outside the Double Musky restaurant thus rendering my spray more of an enticement than a deterrent.

The following day I mushed across the frozen corrugations of the Little Susitna River, stepping on a spiked grill to slow the huskies when we neared bends, letting them rip along the straights where their breath rose like smoke signals. Snow hung from trees like cotton buds and beyond the white wilderness, a humpbacked Mount Susitna basked in a fireball of sunshine.

That afternoon I took a Cessna light aircraft flight across a broad river delta out towards the great ice-cream scoops of the Alaska Range where we followed a series of glaciers up into Mount McKinley, the highest point in the US. As we dipped a wing to make our return, the pilot maliciously informed me, "Not everyone makes it back." He then told me, nodding his head in appreciation about pioneering bush pilot, Don Sheldon: "Don has the record - 26 crashes and he survived them all."

All the people I met in and around Alyeska were equally exceptional. There was Yukon Don, an ex-gold panner and trapper who'd sailed the entire 2,000 miles of the Yukon River and wore a bear skin coat and necklace made from the vertebrae of salmon and the teeth and claws of bears. Don was married to Miss Alaska 1982 who'd just returned from bagging a five-foot bull moose and a six-foot black bear when I met her. Then there was ex-psychiatric nurse Dan Little, who moved out to the bush to work in a bar where he said he got "paid better for seeing the same people". On another occasion, Alison, a fourth generation

Athabascan Indian, proudly showed me a picture of her Russian-speaking grandma dressed in animal pelts holding up two rabbits she'd just trapped. And then there was Jan, a typical incomer, who'd quit her job as an interpreter at the Los Angeles County Jail after meeting her future husband skydiving near McKinley.

And this year? I'm not sure yet. Maybe the Dolomites but I've heard the skiing in Pakistan is really good.

THAMES BAPTISM

Arrested and almost sunk - an English pilgrimage

Riding the tide, London is a flick-book of images. In minutes the unloved £750-million Dome birthday cake with its lopsided never-lit candles gives way to exuberant screeching gulls piping me through the seaport of Greenwich. Down by the jetty are the diminutive *Gipsy Moth* and lumbering tar-black *Cutty Sark*. High above them, in the royal park the red time-ball of the Royal Observatory plummets as it has at 1pm every day since 1833 as a reminder to shipmasters to adjust their chronometers. I look down at my own watch, vibrating on a wrist glued to the tiller. Six minutes slow. I leave it as it is.

At this same moment no doubt, a battery of camera-toting tourists are capturing loved ones straddling the Greenwich meridian, one foot in the western hemisphere and one in the east - irrefutable proof for empire builders that the world expands outwards from Greenwich. The line they straddle marks the zero meridian, the beginning of time. It also marks the beginning of my journey, the casting off from Greenwich Mean Time in search of English slow time.

Where I'm heading, into a spider's web of canals known collectively as "the Cut", I'll have no need of longitude or latitude. On a couple of previous weekends pootling the margins of England by narrowboat, I've already discovered it to be a world no less magical than Alice's, a secret network as powerful as ley lines. The Cut's history, gauged in the British landscape deeper than the chariot tracks left by the Romans, is a hidden garden flashed with kingfishers and traditional narrowboats; a parallel universe ringing with the laughter of water gypsies, the thin cries of bats and the booming Stygian silence of tunnels.

Over the next few months, *Caroline* will carry me on a single continuous figure of eight from Greenwich up through the Midlands and across the Pennines before returning south. What would take fourteen hours to drive in a car will take one-third of a year by narrowboat. The route I travel will be as much James Brindley's dream as my own for it was his eighteenth-century utopian vision of a *Grand Cross* of man-made waterways linking our major cities to the sea via the main navigable rivers of the realm - the Thames, the Severn, Mersey and Trent - that gave wing to the industrial revolution and the current network.

The timing of my journey, it seems, could not be better. The current renaissance of our inland waterways is being heralded as the New Golden Age of the Canals: waterfront cities are being reborn and as many miles of canal are currently re-emerging annually as opened at the height of late eighteenth-century Canal Mania.

Just as I have no need of longitude nor latitude to navigate my course through backdoor England, neither do I need rocket science to operate *Caroline*. To hire a narrowboat, you don't even need a driving licence - you simply aim the pointy end the way you want to go and stop when the canal does for its arcane ritual of lockgating.

Yes, anyone can do it but anyone can just as easily make a complete arse of themselves too. Particularly, if like me, you're sailing solo. As a novice with just a handful of days boating under my belt I dread the crowds attracted to locks spotting me dropping a rope into the drink or smashing into a gate. Mooring has even greater potential for humiliation - attempting not to knock the flower boxes off roofs of parked boats nor scratch freshly painted hulls, while veteran boaters line the banks, arms folded, shaking their heads despairingly at every new display of incompetence. Then of course there's the possibility … probability … of falling in the canal itself.

What's making me anxious at this moment, however, is not locks or mooring. It's the fact I'm doing the toughest stretch - the tidal Thames - first, and according to my Nicholson guidebook *no* hire companies allow their narrowboats onto the river. Well mine did. But what does that say about Adelaide Marine?

Along with the anxiety, and the emotional roller coaster I'm riding by leaving my family, I'm also on the crest of a tsunami of optimism and excitement. A lethal cocktail. And right now things are moving at a pretty hairy pace. In a couple of hours I may well be pootling at 3mph along a tide-less canal with plenty of time for swapping tea bags and chat, but for the time being steering demands constant adjustment, particularly each time *Caroline* is picked up by a powerful slipstream and partially turned.

From beyond the muddied banks of Deptford Creek comes the crunching sound of unwanted cars being pummeled in a breaker's yard. Beyond it stands the seventeenth-century Mayflower pub, named after the ship that sailed from its moorings to invent the modern world. A few hundred yards further on, the waterfront gallery of The Angel overhangs the river. This is where the *Mayflower*'s captain, Christopher Jones, bought supplies and crew, and where Captain James Cook holed up while preparing for his Antipodean adventure.

A police launch skips past, barely touching the water, creating an instant wash of guilt. I always feel guilty in their presence - a legacy of my three years' probation as a delinquent adolescent. A swarm of helicopters buzzes overhead. As I make another long serpentine loop with the river, Tower Bridge soars above me, an airy castle from a children's book across which hordes ebb and flow between work and home. After the Tower comes the architectural stew of the City and the gun-grey menace of HMS *Belfast*. I sail on through sun gulleys with ominous rain clouds stacked on the horizon. On the left, the converted warehouse of Hay's Galleria, where tea clippers once unloaded from India and China, is filled with office workers munching on bagels and sipping lattes in trendy cafés beneath a glass-roof atrium. The pages of the flick-book keep turning.

The wash from *Caroline* funnels across to a small Mississippi mud beach where two boys, aged ten or eleven, are skimming stones from broken pallets beside a half-eaten sheep. Above them stands the preposterously small replica *Golden Hind* in its puddle at the corner of the Old Thameside Inn. Alongside it is a sign - "The World Encompassed 1577-1580." Nearby, a man is sitting on the wall, legs akimbo, blowing on each individual crisp from a Walkers packet as if they're steaming chips, before popping them into his mouth. On the steps down to the mudflats from the Founders Arms, a black man and a white woman are passionately entwined, a yin-yang mandala. It feels wonderfully spring-like and optimistic.

I'm growing in confidence, looking around more, taking in the sites, when suddenly the engine breaks back into consciousness. It's making funny - funny as in strange - noises. Over the next few months I'll learn to be more sensitive to *Caroline*'s moods and complaints. For the time being I try to ignore her belly grumbles.

I start picking up occasional snatches of music, and even loud conversation from the bank. One voice reminds me of a teenage girl I'd heard a week earlier standing outside the Tate Modern screaming at her father, "Where the hell were you? I was worried?" Dads do get lost.

Leading from the Tate Modern, the ethereal Millennium Bridge, the first river crossing in central London for a century, floats above me, its aluminium vertebrae on the move, a giant sci-fi stingray leaping from the water.

The drizzle that has intermittently pattered on the deck becomes more insistent. Clouds have thickened, rain is now hammering down, and the enveloping darkness has transformed the river into steel corrugations. I think back to the illuminated skyline I strolled under a week earlier outside the Tate Modern when a heavenly fire seemed to burn above the city. That was when I first started thinking about omens. What was the saying? Red sky at night shepherd's delight? I don't know if we have shepherds anymore. No doubt I'll find out during the next twenty weeks.

I let go of the tiller and make a snatch for my waterproof. By the time the tiller's back in my hand I'm heading towards the northern bank. Fortunately nothing's coming.

I sail under Hungerford Bridge and Charing Cross Station. Later that evening I read in the *Evening Standard* that just a few hours before I passed it, a train ran amok hitting buffers and gauging a ten-foot hole into the concourse. The country is in the grip of Mad Train Disease after Mad Cow, Mad Weather, Swine Fever and Foot-and-Mouth.

As I approach Westminster Bridge, a police launch does a show-off water plough to bring itself alongside *Caroline*. What have I done? "Work's being carried out on Westminster Bridge," a uniformed man shouts across. My neck muscles relax. "Only one section's open. Follow the green, not the red, arrow."

"But I'm colour blind," I shout back.

The uniform stares long and hard, assessing whether I'm just a loser or trying to take the piss. "Follow the arrow and avoid the cross then. You're not cross blind are you?"

Just as I'm about to pass under the bridge I catch sight of my friend Nick Crane with his battered old Olympus shooting pictures of me and *Caroline*. Once through the far side, I slow and look up again. Nick is waving frantically between camera clicks. I wave back and suddenly my Conradian sense of destiny awaiting in the water margins of England is waylaid by the river police. An inflatable carrying ten frogmen slaloms alongside me. I slow the boat. With the engine purring, I can now hear sirens seemingly coming from every direction, and above me helicopters are playing out scenes from *Apocalypse Now*.

I remember with a shock it's 1 May - May Day. And May Days are not what they once were. The city is heavy with paranoia. Eight hundred demonstrators have gathered on bikes at Kings Cross. In other parts of town anarchists, Greens and common-or-garden anti-capitalist foot soldiers have assembled. Six thousand police officers are on duty and another 3,000 waiting in the wings in case things turn nasty. Buildings have been boarded up and Westminster schools closed for the day. What has most bearing on my own present situation, however, are the hundreds of protesters milling about on the other side of the Houses of Parliament that I am now idling outside.

The frogmen in the inflatable are clearly patrolling the building and spotting an anarchist cyclist on the bridge - Nick - and his mate in the boat - me - exchanging signals beside the seat of the British Government, reasonably enough assume that an attack is imminent.

I smile and raise a hand as greeting. The flat faces circled by sinister rubber hoods are expressionless. I smile some more. Not a flicker. They come in closer and gesticulate that I am to accompany them. I do as I'm told, continuing to grin inanely so they hopefully won't shoot me. Twenty eyes are trained on me, aching to be staring down a barrel.

My new playfriends escort me past the neo-Gothic pinnacles of Parliament, the House of Lords and Westminster Abbey and don't quit until - with another showy turn – I slip beneath Lambeth Bridge.

It's half an hour before I stop looking over my shoulder. The abandoned Battersea Power Station, known the world over to sad Pink Floyd fans, floats past, followed by a 100-foot tall Peace Pagoda with gilded Buddha and wind chimes. *Caroline* sprints between the towers of two medieval parish churches that mark an ancient river crossing at Putney Bridge, and passes a string of rowing clubhouses. Just ahead a boat crewed by six females is powering towards me on the wrong side of the river with only their muscular backs to guide them. Ever the gentleman, I move closer to the bank to accommodate them. Bad mistake.

It's then that I hear for the first time on my four-month odyssey, fingernails being dragged across a blackboard. Thankfully the sound quickly vanishes. Grendel, trying to get in below decks, has moved on. Then the sound returns, just as it has to in every schlock-horror movie. The next time it stops, so does *Caroline*. A swarm of butterflies takes off inside my stomach. The engine panics, straining for escape. But we're going nowhere. A wave hits the side of the boat and Caroline lists ominously.

The river is a bubbling cauldron and there are no other boats about (the rowing crew is probably back in the boathouse now enjoying a cup of tea). I try to accelerate into the centre of the river but we're as beached as the whale I recently read about washed up on a Sussex beach. I try reversing. It seems to work. I'm moving. In reverse, however, it's impossible to have any control over direction and within seconds the sand bar has me again.

I have only just started my great escape from London and already I've been snared. I put the boat into forward gear once more and turn the tiller from side to side. Not an inch. *Caroline* snarls at the amateur at the tiller.

I try poling off the sand bar. The crowd on the bank that had been just two bored construction workers has grown to a couple of dozen gongoozlers who've interrupted their towpath journey for a bit of entertainment and to bear witness to an unfolding disaster in which a boat sinks after an epic struggle and its solo, incompetent occupant is drowned. As they listen to the item on the evening news, they will be able to say to whoever they share their lives with, "I was there. I saw it."

After maybe twenty minutes of deepening despair, I eventually manage, through a sequence of forward and reverse moves, and chance, to manoeuvre *Caroline* so she faces downstream. By putting all my weight on a pole at the stern, I slowly inch back the way we came. Free of the sand bar, I turn in a wide arc upstream and promise *Caroline* there and then never to leave the middle of a river even if the *QE2* suddenly looms above us.

I have now almost been arrested and almost sunk. It's enough for one day.

At Brentford, I pull off the river, following a sign welcoming me to the Grand Union Canal. It's taken three and a half hours to get here from Greenwich. I'm exhausted but still high as a kite. I'm at the end of rivertime and I won't see the Thames again until I'm on the final leg of the journey, travelling downstream from Oxford's dreaming spires.

I enter a short creek and sail straight into Thames Lock, disturbing a woman

n her twenties who's attending flowerboxes lining the wall. It's the last manned/
womanned lockgate I'll encounter until I reach Wigan.

As *Caroline* and I rise from the maelstrom of the river up into the sanctuary
of the Cut, I ask her where I can moor up. "Anywhere you fancy. Pull up along
on the near bank and pop back for a cuppa if you like. I've got another hour till
knock off."

UKULELE 300 CLUB

My little stick of Blackpool rock

The tram rattled, illuminated pumpkins danced in the wind and fairy lights pulsed around guesthouses called Aloha. Lurking in shop windows were Stud Undies, Bonking Sheep and Grow-A-Pecker plants.

When I was a child growing up in Liverpool, my dad would annually drive us up to Blackpool's Illuminations cursing the traffic as we tailgated along the Prom. Every year he'd swear, "Next time we'll either B&B or take the train," and every year we'd be back day-tripping and tailgating.

Nowadays you can buy seaside rock with Arabic or Chinese writing running through it, and the pub opposite the station has been renamed The Flying Handbag, one of a clutch bag of new gay bars. But nothing has *really* changed. The Tower still scratches the arse of the sky, the Pleasure Beach rides roar and you can still get oysters and cockles on the three piers that jut into the sea like Neptune's trident.

As the tram finally drew up outside the Pleasure Beach, my stomach cramped as I caught sight of my favourite ride on the planet, the Pepsi Max Big One. Unfortunately the world's then highest, steepest, fastest rollercoaster wasn't running because of the high winds ("illuminations weather", as the tram conductor put it). So instead I had to make do with bobsleighing down a suspended serpentine wicker run, getting drenched on the log flume and cranking up the adrenaline on the park's five classic wooden rollercoasters. Botticelli clouds lit up the stormy sky as I rocketed around the park, a rollercoaster steeplechaser hurtling towards white horses galloping across the Irish Sea.

To the rollercoaster cognoscenti, going to Blackpool's Pleasure Beach is going to heaven. The Grand National is the ultimate wooden rollercoaster not only because it should soon receive a telegram from the Queen on its centenary. Nor because it is wooden and therefore can both clatter and provide double and triple drops. No, the real reason for its pre-eminence in the rollercoast canon is because it operates on twin tracks, meaning you can hurl insults across at the competing careening carriage as you plummet and soar. American fans make annual pilgrimages to drool over it or to have their marriages blessed.

Its sister, the Big Dipper also has its fans - American school teacher, diabetic and coaster anorak Richard Rodriguez spent three weeks strapped into it to earn his entry in *The Guinness Book of Records*.

But the Pleasure Beach was not the only place in Blackpool where the adrenaline was flowing that weekend as more than 300 George Formbys with ukuleles were descending on the Winter Gardens, intent on galloping through more innuendo in two minutes than Frankie Howerd managed in a lifetime. It was to this, their latest convention, that I hurried the next morning as the resort was still yawning and nursing its daily hangover.

ALASKAN LONELY HEARTS CLUB

As Martin Harrison launched into "With My Little Ukulele in My Hand" with a grin, a suitably cheeky-chappy vocal and a Gatling-gun ukulele style, I experienced an immediate swoop through the loft of childhood. Cigarette cards flickered, brilliantly coloured marbles rolled, and an olfactory trail of Imperial Leather and Brylcreem led me back to Saturday night teatime kippers and Dad spinning his treasured collection of 78s.

Like many of those assembled for the quarterly George Formby convention, I was not around in the master of the *double-entendre*'s 1940s pomp. Nevertheless his recordings and films permeated my sixties Liverpool childhood. It must have been much the same for Beatle George Harrison, who secretly attended a similar convention some years back with his son and confessed that as soon as he finished his Saturday morning butcher delivery duties as a lad, he'd excitedly scoot down to the local flicks with his hard-earned dosh to watch another Formby film. The ex-Beatle knew better than most that before the Liverpool Sound the Formby Sound reigned.

The Formby Society, founded in 1961 (the year Formby died), hosts four Blackpool weekend gatherings a year and all are open to the public. Most of those assembled were Society members. Some had come to buy and sell instruments, others to wallow in nostalgia, but the vast majority had come to play. As they drifted into the Winter Gardens' intimate Theatre Bar, they jotted their name on a list, ensuring each would get to play two Formby songs of their choice over the weekend.

Martin Harrison had been the first up, already a ukulele legend in his mid twenties and with a Formby grin to match. Martin was followed on stage by dad-and-son team Andy and Will Parker, who hurtled through "Mr Wu's a Window Cleaner Now". The enthusiastic audience was casually smart with not a cloth cap in sight. Ages, geographical spread and backgrounds were broad - Andy himself was a surgeon from Matlock.

Young players like Heidi, fifteen (who also played clarinet, cornet and piano) and Adam Smith, nineteen, from Burton-on-Trent and Derby respectively, spoke of Formby as if he were a close personal friend rather than someone who'd died before they were born. Older members such as Jack Jones, aged eighty and now confined to a wheelchair, could still recall the precise moment he heard the master's voice. "I were a young lad in hospital and a nurse had taken a special shine to me and brought me fish and chips each night. One night she brought a radio too. First song I ever heard of George's was "Little Ukulele in My Hand". December 13, 1935. Bingo. I were hooked."

Ukuleles glistened beneath the chandeliers, as Frances Terry, aged 71, fidgeted with her specially made outfit and approached the stage. Earlier she'd confessed to me, "I don't really know why I do it. It's like the dentist's for me every time." But do it she did in her riding boots, red hunting jacket, striped satin waistcoat and top hat. She forgot the lines of "Bunkum's Travelling Show", stumbled over chords and still got one of the biggest cheers of the day. Over the nine years she'd been a Society member, she'd not missed one of the 36 gatherings, once even attending with bronchitis.

As soon as the next act started cantering through "Bunty's Such A Big Girl Now" ("Bunty's such a big girl now, a boat was tattooed on her hip. Bunty's such a big girl now, it's turned into a battleship"), Frances slumped back into her chair exhausted from the nervous excitement and started fretting over which songs she'd learn for the next bash and which costumes she should make to accompany them.

As members continued to hurtle breathlessly through their favourites, I decided to take a break, slipped out of the door and headed for the Blackpool Tower.

In the timelocked heaven of cherubs and gilt that is the Tower Ballroom, I found a similar mix of ages waltzing across the dance floor to a Wurlitzer played by a Reg Dixon lookalike as if the last half century never happened. Locked bodies were gliding effortlessly across the buffed dance floor as Phil Kelsall, rose with his Wurlitzer from the underworld, as he had done most days these past 26 years (and as Reg had done before him for forty years). I felt like I'd somehow slipped inside a French Renaissance jewellery box. Decorating the lid were angelic cherubs clinging to the scalloped roof that nubile caryatids were attempting to lift open. Frank Matcham's masterpiece is considered one of the three finest ballrooms in the land but I find it hard to believe anything else could run it close.

Last time I was here I'd been mesmerised by a septuagenarian with a Shirley Temple ribbon in her hair who was gamely attempting several high kicks of the *paso doble* while her partner clattered his feet round her like castanets. This time my attention was immediately drawn to a diminutive dapper couple, no taller nor heavier than sparrows, who moved as if they were a single body. They also appeared to be totally smitten with each other. When they finally took a breather, I sidled over to the table and struck up conversation.

In life some people find God but Dorothy Middleton aged 66, and Norman Casey, aged 71, found the Blackpool Tower Ballroom early on and never looked back. Both first visited the resort as children: Dorothy from Bradford, Norman from Manchester. They both then returned regularly until they finally, independently, settled in the resort. Norman's wife and original dance partner died of cancer in 1993. Dorothy's husband, stalked by the same killer, followed five years later. Eventually Norman managed to persuade his friend Dorothy to return to the Ballroom.

"It was really hard - so many memories. But it helped," Dorothy remembers "Both our marriages were very happy ones and we'd spent a lot of our lives dancing here."

"There really is no place like the Tower," Norman adds, nodding his head to affirm the special role the ballroom has had in their rehabilitation. "And for Dorothy it's even more important. It's her cathedral. When she was a young girl and her parents asked her where she wanted to go it was always the Tower. Even though we now live in Blackpool, she still isn't interested in going abroad."

"It's an oasis." Dorothy attempts to explain the hold the place has over her. "When you go out the building, there's all sorts going on, but inside here nothing fades. Blackpool Tower." She shakes her head. "Nothing like it. You'll probably think us mad, but when they decided to replace the old carpet surrounding the dance floor I asked for a piece and I've framed it and have it up on my wall next to a photograph of the pier."

The couple conjure up images of those other made-for-each-other dancing fantasists Ginger Rogers and Fred Astaire and I can resist the question no longer. "So are you…" I stumble for words that will convey my question but not in so indelicate a manner as to embarrass them… "romantically connected?"

Dorothy smiles as innocently as Doris Day. "We are…" she too is seeking the right words, "…just very close friends."

"But we do spend virtually all our time together now," says Norman muddying the water.

Whether they are intimate or not, they clearly have itchy feet. They excuse themselves and join their friends Mike and Jean, who are theatrically high kicking their way through a rumba. Dorothy's left hand clasps Norman's right, while the latter's left hand slinks round her back and she in turn rests her left hand lightly on Norman's shoulder as they float off again across the dancefloor.

I thought back to the church of St Stephen-on-the-Cliffs I'd visited a couple of days earlier where, in the Actor's Chapel, I'd stared at a marble reredos depicting David carrying the Ark of the Covenant back into Jerusalem pursued by a troupe of Blackpool's music hall stars led by Gracie Field.

It suddenly struck me that what the high drama of the Anglican liturgy at St Stephen's shared with the entertainment at the Tower Ballroom, the seasonal promenade theatres and the Formby Society concerts, was an old-fashioned notion of participation. Blackpool itself was just an extension of the extended family sing-along in the parlour, ageless and classless.

Just before I headed back into the Winter Gardens for more music and a Formby film, I hopped on a bus down to St Ann's where George Formby spent much of his life. On the high street outside the Bradford & Bingley Bank I discovered Charles Stewart (who ran the Blackpool branch of the Formby

Society), wife Eve and a few friends - including one aged nine - busking with their ukes. On a whim, I asked Charles where the word ukulele originated. "It's Hawaiian. The word breaks down into two parts 'uku' - which means flea - and 'lele', to dance."

Who knows if it's true? One of the songs Charles sang also claimed that the pyramids were built by the Irish. Whatever, it sums up the music perfectly - the dance of the flea. "It's all to do with how fast the hand moves strumming the strings," Charles continued, "but in Blackpool we really play that fast to avoid frostbite."

Back inside the Theatre Bar at the Winter Gardens, Dennis Mitchell, the MC was chivvying performers along. Next up was a nine-piece all-women ukulele band from Gothenburg who received rapturous applause for their own composition ("Ukulele Ladies") as well as their rendition of Formby's "Swim Little Fish". An hour later, more than thirty Formby Society members crowded the stage for the traditional two-minute "thrash" that closed the concert. On stage I recognised Joe Hodgkin, aged 72, who only took up the uke three years ago. Will (twelve) and Andy Parker were there, and so were Martin Harrison, Heidi, Adam and Frances. In front of the stage stood a large photograph of their hero winking appreciatively.

Back on the front I slipped back a curtain into the crystal-ball-and-tarot-card boudoir of Leah Petulengro. Having had her palm lined with silver, Leah stared into my face as if trying to read a map with bad eyesight. She wrinkled her nose. "I can see that you're going to become more and more successful the older you get." A smile followed before it was wiped clean when she picked up on my singularly unimpressed expression. "In two months' time, you'll make a major decision but don't worry, whatever you decide will be the right course." If only life was like that - no wrong turnings.

Leah had been applying happy balm to Blackpool Prom visitors for half a century. And like horses that occasionally romp home at 100:1, sometimes she even gets it right. When Karen Kay worked a season as an impressionist on the front in the 1970s Leah predicted that her tiny son would become massively rich and famous. Jay Kay now heads Jamiroquoi. Leah also told Johnny Ball that his young daughter Zoe (a local girl) would enjoy similar success.

Later that night, the fog rolled in off the Irish Sea to swallow cars and pedestrians. A clanging announced the arrival of another tram. On board I finally put my reserve aside and joined in with everyone else being led in a gutsy sing song by the conductor. The tram became a moving party, chips shared, cans passed. I can't quite remember whether the songs were from the Formby canon but I wouldn't be at all surprised for Blackpool was made for George just as lampposts were made for leaning on.

V FOR VICTORY

Nashville wannabes

As the electronic window of the cab descended, I immediately recognised the large man with goatee, black leather tie, stetson and cowboy boots. "You're Hank Williams."

The urban cowboy smiled broadly. "Y'all think I bear a resemblance?"

Hank was in fact Dave - Dave Street - and Dave was coincidentally about to launch a Hank Williams Junior show in Nashville. Well, he had earned the words and was recruiting a band and was looking for a theatre where he could charge tourists $5 a time... Meanwhile, he was driving to earn some cash.

Propped up alongside Dave was a guitar he claimed to have bought from Billy Cox, who played bass with Jimi Hendrix's Band of Gypsies. "We were playing in New York together... I was playing in a church, Jimi was playing Madison Square Garden. We became good friends and Jimi was gonna make me rich by recording a couple of my songs."

"What went wrong?" I asked.

"He died."

Nashville runs on the adrenaline of such near-misses. Every newly arrived wannabe and every old drunk with a song scrawled on the back of a fag packet shares the same dream: one day his name will be up in lights and the bank manager will be off his back.

By the end of the ride I'd bought Dave's guitar for $70 and he'd thrown in the case for free.

At Boot Country, on Music Valley Drive, I bought cowboy boots, shirt, hat and bolo for a grand total of $150. God knows why - I hate the stuff. But maybe it had something to do with Jean and Jamie, the shop assistants, singing a duet of Tammy Wynette's "D.I.V.O.R.C.E" while they helped me spend the money. Tammy, now on her fifth marriage, may offer a more poignant rendering, but what Jean and Jeannie lacked for in experience they more than made up for in enthusiasm.

The girls liked singing - they'd been in an all-female group in school - but they were "not so serious as the boss - he's in a band and might be giving up the shop." In LA resting actresses wait on tables; in Nashville resting singers and songwriters wait on tables and run shops, the post office and just about anything else.

For $18 you can record your own single at the You're The Star recording studio on Second Avenue. The staff here do a little talent spotting for a local producer and told me that in the past year they'd sent him three hopefuls. Having mauled my way through Roger Miller's "King of the Road", I smiled at them expectantly when I went to collect my tape. They advised me to stick with my day job.

Not all Limeys take their advice. At Gruhn's, the guitar shop where th
guitar heroes shop, I found Steve, sporting a Liverpool FC top and agonisin
over a purchase. His was the usual problem shoppers at Gruhn's wrestle wit
if he bought the Rickenbacker, he'd only have enough cash left for two week
more rent in town.

Steve had already spent three weeks knocking on doors. He thought he'd b
able to sell his songs; no one wanted them. He thought he'd get gigs in the ba
and support himself with tips but hadn't got a single booking. He'd even trie
busking in Memphis, but was quickly moved on.

Steve would buy that sixties Rickenbacker for $1,800, of that I had no doub
but there was resignation in his voice - he only grew animated when discussing h
other beloved, Liverpool FC. Steve was perilously close to throwing in the towel.

Standing beside a row of seductively sparkling dobros (etched steel on bras
nickel-plated guitars), the shop assistant, Derek, summed up the mini-traged
awaiting the likes of Steve. "The story's always the same. The guy comes i
mooches, asks which guitar Dylan or Clapton bought, mooches some more
leaves, returns an hour or a day later and eventually buys. Within two month
he's back and begging to resell the guitar for half what he paid, to meet some ren
demand or buy a ticket home." The long row of guitars in the pawn shop nex
door was further evidence of broken dreams.

At a local print shop, the manager Jim Sherraden, told me he had enquirie
from "up to twenty kids a week wanting 'the cheapest possible poster'", eithe
to publicise small local gigs they were playing or merely to draw attention t
themselves by plastering their name around. "I do a run of around sixty fo
maybe thirty to forty bucks - don't make nothin' - but I see it as a public service.

Plenty of others who *have* made it are unwittingly supporting those on th
way up. The night before my visit, the stadium rockers ZZ Top had called in
taken Jim out to dinner ("They're real nice boys") and ordered $10,000 wort
of artwork.

Getting that first break is, of course, the hardest thing of all. The Bluebir
Café, the best showcase for new talent, is almost as hard to break into as th
Grand Ole Opry itself. When a set is in progress, talking is forbidden. At ope
night, up to 150 songwriters and singers put their name in a hat. The ones pulle
out get the chance to play. If they're good, they're invited back to play twice mor
on regular show nights. If the audience like them they might even get paid on
day. It's not so long ago that Garth Brooks, the hottest property in Nashvill
when I visited, was trying out material here. Dream on.

The Bluebird may be the country chapel, but Ryman Auditorium is th
"Mother Church of Country Music" where the audience even sits in pews. Th
night I was in the audience, a chunky nineteen-year-old named Mandy Barnet

was pretending to be Patsy Cline, the queen of country who died in a plane crash while still in her thirties. Mandy had struck lucky, Patsy had struck out. In Nashville you are magic or you are tragic; there is no in between. A version of this simple truth was spelt out in neon outside a strip joint on Demonbreun Street: "50 beautiful girls and three ugly ones."

The Grand Ole Opry, which transmitted the nation's longest-running radio show, remains the the biggest dream. But when it outgrew Ryman's, its original home, and moved in the 1970s to a 4,424-seat site out of town many believe it lost its soul.

At Ryman's even Elvis was among the hopefuls (legend has it that at his 1954 audition he was advised to stick to truck-driving). Now the Friday and Saturday night shows stick to a safe roster of mega stars: Loretta Lynn, Ricky Skaggs, Randy Travis. I'd been warned that it was the Wembley Arena of country and it turned out be just as uninspiring.

Like others seeking the real thing, I headed to the honky-tonk chapels on Broadway, where most hopefuls end up playing for tips. At Roberts there were cowboy boots for sale, a long bar, a small dance floor and an even smaller stage. From the latter an elderly picker was singing "She's got the goldmine, I've got the shaft" to an audience of two.

Next door at Tootsies Orchid Lounge, Jimmy Probst II was picking his way through "Ring of Fire", which Johnny Cash had written in the same bar about the time Jimmy's father was born. Jimmy, too, was playing for tips, but at midday he still hadn't made enough for lunch and the signs weren't good. There were four in the audience: two bar workers and a sixty-year-old resident drunk by the name of Walter Raines plus me. Walter also had aspirations. "I'm a songwriter. Have been since I was twelve," he slurringly divulged. "Only just gettin' started though."

"Why?" I asked.

"'Cos it takes longer when you've been drunk for thirty years." Being drunk, apparently, goes with country territory. "Willie Nelson got so drunk here one night he tried to fling himself under a truck outside," Walter fondly reminisced. Walter did not want to go the same way, and his eyes grew rheumy as he shared his dream: "Gonna dry out and get me enough money to buy a gold Cadillac to get buried in."

Maybe Walter will get lucky. The night before my visit, John Michael Montgomery, who recently had a big hit with "I Swear", called in and offered to pay the picker on stage $25 for every Hank Williams song he knew. When it reached 600 bucks, John emptied his wallet, pleaded "no more" and headed home.

It was time for me to be heading that way too. I dropped $5 into Jimmy's box and hailed a cab for the airport. My driver's name was Dee Tucker. He was fitting in a couple of hours at the wheel between teaching music at a local high school and playing a gig at a wedding. Sometimes he played in a jazz trio, sometimes "quieter sterrrf and sometimes jackass five-piece country-kickin' style". In a town where there are more dreamers than there are rhinestones on a cowgirl, a guy just has to know how to mix it.

W THE WHITE STUFF

In search of miracles

lready nauseous from the tightly coiled bends that the driver had driven into with malicious intent, catching sight of the resort of Flaine was enough to make my stomach give up the struggle and boke over my neighbouring passenger. Somehow I held on and quickly averted my eyes from the nasty spillage of cement on the hillside whose ugliness was so perfect that the French had placed a conservation order on it. Even the town's name - Flaaaiiine - suggested eructation. Dressed in a white overcoat, it might just be bearable but in its current snowless state nothing could redeem its unmitigated awfulness. Not that it's any more awful than La Plagne/Les Deux Alpes and the rest of the other purpose built French ski stalags. Why on earth do people come here to ski when they can go to Austria? Probably because they might meet Kurt Waldheim.

The Hotel Aujon fitted the resort like a ski glove in its remorseless functionalism. My cramped bedroom's white stucco walls interrogated with gestapo lighting beneath a sauna heat; there was not a plug socket to be found and the only towels came flannel-sized.

Throwing open the window, I heard small voices drifting up alongside the percussion of ski boots on gravel. I headed down to the bar to join the rest of the group who'd signed up for the "Learn to ski powder" week. Once we'd introduced ourselves, I struck up conversation with the square peg the others had turned their back on. John - chronically stiff and pucker with neat grey hair flecked black, a neat white roll neck and neat blue ski suit - informed me he was interested "in technique over speed…" John then underlined the point, "I seek neatness in all things." John was a linguist ("I speak five and a half languages fluently"). John was a Russian specialist at the MOD (nod nod wink wink). John had brought a notebook to our "get acquainted" evening. John did the football pools by standing order. John talked at me of the tangential stress of boots and the importance of the softness of skis.

Stuart Adamson, our group leader, saved me by suggesting we head down to the ski shop to get kitted out. Here John fiddled and flapped with equipment and splurged statistics as he correlated snow conditions with suitable skis - "Think I'll take a hard surface as I don't think we'll be doing much powder… I might try the new Dynastar Omegas." Good. Go and try them. Take them to bed with you. Park them somewhere warm during the cold night.

Back in the hotel bar two bronzed pilots from the RAF waved a bottle of red at me and proffered a seat. I quickly discovered they were part of a 1,200-strong invading army ("We get the best rates at the end of January when half the rooms are empty") which had already lost 37 of its contingent to serious injury. Within minutes the bottle was empty and so in return for their largesse I used my poor

French to negotiate the minefield of Anglophobic waiters. The second bottle slipped them over the precipice and I left them cursing their former wives and respective alimony settlements.

Upstairs I watched snow falling from my open window. In a field people moved in slow motion across an ice rink. "Sympathy for the Devil" played. I certainly sympathised if this was the mountain mirador he tried to tempt Jesus from. But then, under the stars and mute white peaks, Flaine for a second attained a state of beauty before more dirgey Rolling Stones, as worn and crappy as the lower pistes, crackled over the loudspeakers and ruined things.

There are those who make pretty patterns on the piste, look unbelievably cool and then go to bed with each other. And then there's the rest of us. We sign up one year and we hurry back the next. Then we start to wonder why we're not skiing like our instructor and the people on TV. We miss a season, we may even miss two, but then we're back. We always come back. Ineluctably drawn by visions of balletic transformation, we pay once more, often with an arm and a leg, to listen to the same absurdities from our instructors: "imagine there's a jam sandwich between your shin and your boot"; "imagine you are pressing grapes under your heel"; "imagine, as you make your turn, you are going through a window" ... "going through a door" ... "offering someone an ice-cream" ... "a glass of champagne".

All we want to do is look like them, bugger the sandwiches. But as Stuart Adamson, our instructor pointed out to me the next morning, "I spend 28 weeks a year on the piste. How many do you?" But we - and by we I mean the boys - will feel comfortable retiring to our Valhalla Retirement Home only after we have surfed the Hawaiian Pipe, climbed Everest in a t-shirt and without oxygen (why not without air?) ... and, top of the list, mastered the powder stuff (I mean off-piste, not lines of coke which anyone can do).

So this was to be the year I would transform myself. The year I took the course that converted me from career intermediate into a god of powder complete with wings of spindrift snow. This year I and seven others were to be granted entry to ski nirvana through the hell-hole of Flaine.

The omens, however, weren't good. No snow for a month until a minor fall the night before. Bare rocks lower down. It was beginning to look like being more of a learn-to-ski-ice-and-avoid-the-boulders week.

As I made my way to the lift, spring had arrived on the slope despite it not yet being February. The grass had turned from mangy brown to proud green on the lower slopes and the sun was beaming as if enjoying its first day instead of its zillionth year on the job. As my course wasn't starting until the following morning, I headed off in search of ski legs.

The first fall happened behind me as I entered the cable car. I turned, praying it was the young girl who'd learnt to whistle at breakfast and had been tunelessly practising in my lughole again as we queued for the lift. It wasn't unfortunately. It was one of the air force pilots from the night before. "Slipped on my fucking boot strap."

At the summit, a helicopter buzzed overhead and I expected the "Ride of the Valkyries" to explode from loudspeakers as it set off to scoop up another early casualty. The manic whir of the medic chopper would return several more times that morning as I pootled and hurtled in my usual directionless fashion reaffirming my love-hate relationship with the slopes. One minute I was Jean-Claude Killy, or whoever is the current equivalent, and the next I was clattering out of control. A common or garden day for the veteran intermediate.

Miraculously that night snow began to fall with more serious intent and when I awoke the next morning, it was still falling. After the blistering heat of the day before, it almost seemed staged.

I met up with the rest of our group, half of whom came from Manchester and were already bragging to each other about the alcohol they were going to chuck down their throats on the slopes to prove that they were manly, muscular and overflowing with sperm. Our token female, Karen, worked in an intensive care unit in Stockport. Handy. She and Andrew had a twenty-month-old daughter they had left at home with Grandma. Andrew sold cars, Kirk sold computers and Phil sold houses. None were selling very much. As is the way when boys form groups, Kirk was quickly and silently designated the sacrificial lamb. It was Kirk we offered first to the mountain when things looked tricky, and it was Kirk we would look to for consolation when skiing badly ("Well at least I ski better than Kirk"). Someone has to be the repository of the group anxiety and Kirk appeared a willing enough victim. As we ascended the mountain on the first day of our course, Kirk told me that the year before he'd been heliskiing in New Zealand. How he survived is no less a miracle than Jesus' conversion of water into wine.

Apart from our four Mancunians, there was Tony, a fifty-year-old antiques dealer from Chelsea (not selling much) and Malcolm, a 23-year-old who served behind the bar in the Aberdeen students' union (selling a lot). And then there was Square Peg John who entered conversations obliquely and left them similarly. John. Who when we had a snowball fight, pointed out, "Do you know no two snowflakes are the same?" as he got one in the mouth.

At 47, Stuart Adamson, our instructor, was playing out our fantasies. The silver-haired legend of the slopes with a penchant for rave cotton trousers had sat at the bar the night before with his young girlfriend, their legs entwined like vines in Eden. At first his jokes and garrulousness had suggested a shallowness to equal the snow on the lower slopes but, I reasoned, he couldn't be that daft getting paid to ski as well as extra-curricular perks.

At the top of the mountain, visibility was down to the inch between our distended eyes. We tried to keep a tight crocodile, arms further out than usual as if trying to ski in braille. Karen unfortunately fell awkwardly on one of our first runs, broke a thumb and had to return home for an operation or else risk losing the grip in her right hand. That was the end of our token female.

My own skiing that first day was awful. And then I got worse. As all skiers know, awfulness is a slippery slope. Three of us were dreadful while the other three, tentatively at first, got their bounce technique going and grew to Zarathustrian heights by the end of day which only further increased our sense of wretchedness. Kirk decided he'd start chipping notches on his skis for the number of people he'd wiped out.

An army of caterpillar daleks appeared over the brow of the hill hissing their alien gutturals, whirling lights and attacking the piste. Cloud came and went; dramatic gobs of sun suddenly illuminated peaks. Somewhere here there was drama and beauty, I knew, but my boots hurt and I was miserable. Wasn't it Byron who said, "Love cannot withstand seasickness"? Well beauty cannot withstand broken spirits and feet. What's more I hated Stuart who was hugely irritating (why was he being so bloody encouraging and nice?). As we headed back onto the piste from a coffee break, three snowboarders in grunge uniform zoomed past. "Gays on trays," Stuart shouted after them; "Pricks on sticks," one bright spark threw back and I laughed unnaturally loudly.

The second day, of course, was glorious. The lift hovered over the great white belly of the mountain, stretch marks fanning where small slides had occurred. At the top, cloud bubbled up the far valley beneath the gnarled peaks. The trees, liberally dipped in caster sugar, looked like decorations on a birthday cake. *Now* it was beautiful. Soon we were off making fresh tracks, the dream of all ski addicts and I was a Titan on the slopes. Stuart wasn't irritating at all. He was a superb instructor - the best I'd ever had. He was witty, full of insight and could probably climb Everest without air.

As we stood under a huge outcrop of rock ("Perfect avalanche material" Stuart drily observed) with virginal powder spread before us, the slope sparkled like expensive jewellery. Stuart stopped and sighed. "D'you know I'd rather share this than all the real diamonds in the world." The group shared his excitement, all made good progress and enjoyed one of those days you dream about around November when nights draw in and winter spreads before you like a heavy wet blanket.

But, later that day as we re-joined the piste from the powder, Kirk inexplicably hurtled into a rock and his knee popped out. A doctor back in the resort popped it back but it ballooned up like a football and that, unfortunately, was the end of Kirk who would now spend the rest of the week propped up in

Flaine's bars. We were devastated. Who now would be the lamb? I detected hint of a smile lurking on the others' faces.

That night the hotel restaurant was as noisy and bright as Luton airport One particularly boisterous group from Jersey burst into "Here we go, her we go, here we go". Where they were going I could not fathom. Meanwhile larger group of Germans lumbered through "Über Alles" and an internationa repertoire that included "My Bonnie Lies Uver the Ucean" and "Una Palom Blanca". The songs were virtually indistinguishable, delivered as a bottomles dirge peppered with heavy Germanic glottal stops. The Mancunians ran a bool on whether Kirk had the bottle to send a gob of creamy cake over his shoulde towards an impressively stacked woman in low slung halter top. This was aprè ski.

By Wednesday we hardly noticed the Ortovoxes strapped to our chests tha hopefully would call the cavalry if we were swallowed by an avalanche. Eas confidence filled our chests as we discussed the woman from St John's Wood wh had sailed off a cliff in Austria a fortnight before. None of us could understan it. Stuart called up to me, "Paul, cross the tracks I've left to make a chain ... an make sure you stop this side of me." I hurtled several feet beyond him and jus managed to stop in front of a ten-foot drop. John sailed over it.

But today it was the turn of Tony, who was on his second "learn to sk powder" week, to really struggle. "My father skied to school in Austria everyda as a boy and at 52 I'm still attending ski school!"

On Thursday morning my body faced down the slope, arms were forward only my lower body moving, feet on the middle of the skis, ankles rolling an I was squashing those jam sandwiches. Well, maybe. I looked back at my track which I felt should be sculpted and put in the Tate. In the afternoon, of cours everything fell apart again. I was sitting back, pushing the skis and getting n bounce (bloody instructors).

The week's skiing was a switchback: one day it was scorching and I wa skiing through a milkshake; the next I was zipping through fresh snow. One da my spirits soared and the next they were dashed.

Is it something perverse that draws us back or simply that we prefer t remember only those moments of success and exhilaration? Are we simpl driven? Unable to accept mortality? You tell me. But when it all clicks, the turn come, the ankles roll and I even manage a bounce or two, I really don't care. Th sun shines, there's a big cheesy smile on my face and, heavens, a plume of powde like an angel's wings is following behind me.

Loved up on the The Daly Love Trail

ALASKAN LONELY HEARTS CLUB

In Lisdoonvarna I was informed that William Daly was the man to sort me out. "Everybody knows Willie - he's responsible for just about every marriage in town … and just as many divorces. He'll be in the Matchmaker's tonight for sure."

That evening, a barman at the Matchmaker Bar kindly pointed William's blaze of white hair bobbing around the dance floor, doing the rounds, making gentle introductions, carrying a bunker-sized ledger under his arm like a racetrack bookie. I decided it wasn't the right moment to approach while he was conducting business. A woman eating a sandwich in a corner of the room between dances provided me with a little more Willie background. "He's been the matchmaker in these parts for forever. Before him it was his father and before him it was his grandfather. Now his daughter Marie is learning the ropes." I finished my pint and left Willie to his work; my own enquiry was less pressing and could wait until the morning.

It was Daly's own soft Irish brogue that duly answered the phone. "You're most welcome to join our present Love Trail group tomorrow if you like. You'll have some catching up to do, mind, as they've already had several days in the saddle. They're a small friendly bunch so you shouldn't feel like a trout at a wedding."

Finding the Carraig Mountain Love Trail proved to be as elusive as romance itself. Eventually I stumbled on a crudely painted sign - "Pony trekking 4 kilometres" - and arrived just as Willie was parking his Nissan Bluebird at the farm he and his father before him had grown up on. Following introductions, Willie ruffled his full white beard while his sheepdog, Rosie, jumped amorously up my leg. Apparently there would be a delay. My fellow love-struck equestrians had had a bit of a session the night before. "Didn't get away from the Matchmaker until three so they'll be a little tardy today."

While I sat on a whitewashed wall and waited, I watched Willie getting a ten-strong family party from Leeds off on a two-hour hack. None of the group had ridden before. The male head of the family, astride Pamela Anderson ("She'll get you off in the right mood"), handed over the money and Willie granted his benediction: "May your luck and wealth prosper together equally and you give birth to a bishop." One young woman was apprehensive; Mel Gibson, her steed, seemed a little skittish. "Don't worry we had an 83-year-old woman here a few weeks back and Mel was her first ride too," Willie encouraged improbably.

Willie's son Harry led the equestrian learners on his push bike as they set off for a nearby lake and haunted house. When they were out of earshot I asked Willie whether it was true about the 83-year-old. "Sure it is. She was on her honeymoon with her new 23-year-old husband, a group leader on her previous holiday – botany, I think it was, on Easter Island. Can't imagine she learnt much though - the man never opened his mouth once when he was here."

Willie smoothed a crumpled letter from his top pocket. It had arrived that morning and was from a French pilot requesting a place on a Love Trail in a month's time. "Foreign men like the honesty and patience of Irish women. Unfortunately Irish women don't appreciate the qualities of Irish men…" Willie's eyes twinkled… "So it's a good job foreign women do."

Willie then told me a typical case of a couple arriving as strangers and leaving as lovers. "They turned up independently and I could tell straightaway they were right for each other. I gently kept them together on the trail. The man from Limerick was very keen but the German girl was shy. One night we were camping out high on the Burren and a terrible thunderstorm broke out. The man checked to see if the girl was alright. She invited him into her tent and that was that. They returned a few months ago actually on a second horse-riding holiday, but this time they were husband and wife. The man plays with an Irish band in Munich now."

When my group finally shuffled in, they shared the easy intimacy that comes with having spent time together in the saddle. Willie made the introductions. Esther was from Wimbledon, Barry from Mitcham. Both were in their forties. Vanessa, from Redcar, was twenty. Patricia from Oklohoma - but now resident in County Clare - was 47 but looked to be in her early thirties. Sean, who was to lead the hack, was a 39-year-old local single farmer.

Our posse of Connemaras and Irish Hunters got into file and exited the farm past Rosie as she kept cavey on the wall. I was on a pale dappled grey bizarrely called Black Beauty. Willie rarely rode out these days, leaving the riding to his daughter Marie, Patricia or Sean. He instead met up to work his magic with the group in the evenings. All the nights so far, according to Barry, had been the equal of the previous evening's marathon session. As we gently ambled down the lane, Barry ran me through a catalogue of memorable songs he'd heard over the week in a bevy of musical pubs. One was a honeymoon tune, "Mary cut your toenails or you will tear the sheets", performed in Gus O'Connor's in Doolin. Then there was the local complicated reel called "The cow ate the blanket".

As we sauntered, the tales and machinations of the previous days unravelled. Vanessa had come openly seeking romance. She loved Ireland, loved the farm and reputedly had designs on one of Willie's sons. I say reputedly because over the next five hours on the trail Vanessa never once stopped whispering sweet nothings to her pony, Misty.

Barry had been "a good friend" of Esther's for fifteen years and was eager to marry her, but she was resistant. He hoped the romance of the trail might seduce her but there was little sign of it. Most interesting of all, however, was Willie's own recent history which I soon started piecing together. It transpired that Patricia-from-Oklohoma had smitten Willie nine months earlier at a set dance and they had been an item ever since ("You have to bear in mind, Paul, Willie has all the flannel - remember he's responsible for literally thousands of marriages," Barry explained). Chainsmoking Sean, like Vanessa, was also seeking romance. Unfortunately, he confided, he tended to get cold feet. He shook his head knowingly, perhaps remembering the fate of friends, "Love is blind but marriage is an eye opener."

The countryside of Clare, like the intrigues, unravelled gently. It has, of course, its share of mysteries - dry lakes suddenly filled, the wind-whispered tales of an old abandoned soup kitchen, a white thorn tree standing alone in a field, a large rock inexplicably balancing on a slender stone pillar.

From the saddle on the Burren's "green roads" (originally used to drive cattle), the views over Galway Bay all the way to the Bens of Connemara could have made Clement Freud gush. Over the hills, zippered with grey stone walls, we continued at a leisurely trot. With no sealed roads and only the very occasional walker, it is a landscape tailor-made for the foreplay of horse riding.

We passed Christian monasteries, high crosses and nibbled castles perfect for marriages and honeymoons. Foals gambolled, herons lumbered and sun buttered the grass like it only can in God's own country.

Soon the sex moved up a gear as we gave rein and galloped along a deep sandy beach which led to a pub, Ireland's post-coital equivalent of the cigarette. We dismounted in the seafront car park and sat on the wall holding reins whilst Sean ferried drinks and sandwiches from O'Looneys. Vanessa continued to coo with Misty and then with Barry. I, meanwhile, stared out to sea to wet-suited boys riding white foam on their stiff boards.

That night in Willie's own Daly's Bar in Ennistymon, we discovered Vanessa had hidden talents: she was a fortune teller. With the help of Barry's watch and Esther's crucifix, she predicted they would marry on 16 May "in a year or two" and that they would move back to Esther's roots (both Esther's parents are Irish).

It sounded unlikely. Over the fifth or six glass of wine Esther whispered in my ear, "It's not worth risking spoiling a great relationship when it took me so long getting out of my last one." Will Vanessa find love in Ireland? Maybe... She was to leave for Redcar the following day but is planning to come back in the summer to help Willie... *and the boys*. Will Patricia and Willie last? With that beauty wrapped round them, why not? And will Sean find true love? Maybe.

As we rode out of town following lunch, we passed a woman walking down a lane and Sean confessed in a whisper, "Felt like I got hit by lightnin'. Something happened. I felt real shaky." For the next half hour I watched Sean shaking his head side to side trying to understand his unsettling experience. Eventually he suggested we stop at another pub for a beer to calm him down. Three minutes later the same woman walked through the door. Sean's Aphrodite was from Germany and was studying English in Galway. They talked easily and fixed a date for the following Monday. Sean nervously sought reassurance from the rest of the group who'd witnessed the fledgling romance. "Do you think she was pretty?" Everyone nodded and mumbled their approval. Sean smiled and lit a cigarette off the last one. "Maybe I'll be lucky in love. After all I'm forty on February 14 - not many have their birthday on Valentine's Day."

YUK

Gunned down in the Korean oil drum diner

The host at our lodge seemed a little crazy. For 600 years Kyongju had reigned as the capital of the Silla kingdom, perhaps the highest expression of Buddhist culture the world had ever seen, and for all 600 of them our host had been sitting cross-legged in his raised rabbit hutch at the heart of his home. As we smiled and moved a large petrol can to facilitate our exit into town, he lowered his book. "By Emile Bell. Top restaurant. 500 wan discount." He raised an index finger and then twitched the hand to his right. He then raised two fingers on the other hand and twitched to the left. "First right, second left?" I sought confirmation from my wife. Her half nod, half shake of the head claimed neutrality on the subject no doubt so I could be later blamed for steering us wrong. The lodge owner then handed me a voucher with what appeared to be an address in the top left corner before shooshing us out the door.

After a couple of wrong turns - it transpired the instructions were for a second left and first right - we eventually found the right street and number. The only problem was that the shutters were down to the floor and it appeared to be a garage. As my stomach had been growling for several hours, I banged on the aluminium door and heard a shuffling inside. Rats? Eventually the shutter rose and an ancient, slippered crone appeared and gave me a goofy smile as she grabbed me round the waist and tried to march me into what I had now been able to confirm was indeed a garage (the give away was the numerous petrol cans, bundles of newspapers and an old ironing board).

I shook my head wildly and retreated in an attempt to close on my wife who had already broken into a canter down the street. The woman, however, was in hot pursuit, yelling "Emile, Emile" as she gesticulated wildly. Susanna stopped suddenly. "A meal?"

"Emile," the woman repeated, nodding her head vigorously. My wife in turn nodded and led us back to the garage.

Once inside, the woman lowered the shutters on what remained of daylight. Soon, no doubt, I would feel the blade under my ribs. In the darkness I could see a glow emanating from another room which turned out to be the innocuous glow of three burning oil drums and the alcoholic flush of two middle-aged Koreans. The woman cleared a few fish skeletons from a perforated stone slab covering the third oil drum and motioned us to sit. We smiled across to the two men who gummily grinned back and swayed from behind a joint total of no more than five or six teeth. We smiled again. They continued to grin. This was going to be painful.

"American, American," the first drunk suggested.

"No, we're English," we clarified. He nodded knowingly and congratulated himself on his perspicacity with a nod, "American". His slightly less drunk friend then pointed at us, "Polish." He then clacked his fingers together like castanets and shook his head to indicate he had no command of the language. More Drunk now commenced rat-a-tat-tatting behind an imaginary machine gun. Less Drunk pointed to his companion, "Vietnam… Frenchish."

"Boom. Rat-a-tat-tat," More Drunk continued. I whispered to Susanna, "I think he fought against the French in Vietnam."

"I'm not going to eat," she replied apropos of nothing. She has never shared my anxiety about upsetting local sensibilities. It would be difficult to suggest we'd just popped in for an MOT but forgotten the car and so I resigned myself to eating alone.

What the guesthouse owner had promised as some kind of Asian culinary highpoint was to leave me permanently scarred and still suffering Post Traumatic Stress Disorder. Following this meal, anything vaguely olfactorily resembling the aroma of burning car tyres, sugar refineries or dentists' old rubber masks starts my stomach heaving.

The woman brought out ten small dishes which she arranged round the perimeter of my bonfire. The first, a slither of dried fish, turned out to be a mouthful of fin. More Drunk pointed to the seaweed: "Number one, number one." Less Drunk joined in: "Korea number ten." In another dish my pork, noodles and cardboard sausage were bubbling nicely like a chemistry experiment. More Drunk by now had rolled up his trouser leg and with more sound effects was demonstrating how a bullet whistled through it. Not wishing to be caught with his trousers down, he quickly rolled the material down again and resumed manning his machinegun post, simultaneously yelling, "America. Vietnam." I reappraised my initial conclusion, "I think he fought for the Americans in Vietnam."

I tried to suppress my retching while continuing to force more garage delicacies down. Susanna had her own work cut out trying to suppress her giggles before maliciously asking, "What's it like?"

I held down another boke and found a suitable analogy: "like a rubber jockstrap stir-fried in sick."

There seemed to me something calculated, something planned by someone somewhere, about the whole evening from the initial press ganging and the sharpened chopsticks right through to Less Drunk's obvious pleasure in warning me before each new dish. "Hot, hot, very hot." It was hot, very hot, but heat was not the real problem. The problem was that this was foulness like foulness never before imagined.

When I finally managed to scoop up some unknowable red muck that must have been dead at least 1,200 years and probably recovered from the nearby Silla kingdom ruins, More Drunk ripped into more Viet Cong. I felt like Winston Smith as they lowered the rat cage over his head. Next up more imitation spinach and tripe. My stomach again lurched at the betrayal. Nearly. Hold on. My grin and bear it stoicism finally cracked and I pushed away the final two dishes before paying as-fast-as-possible.

Later that evening, as we crossed an icy street in a snow storm, Susanna slipped and crashed to the pavement, smashing all the biscuits she'd just bought for her supper. I allowed myself a roar of laughter unnaturally loud and refused to help her up.

ZEN AND THE ART OF BALANCE

Hog on the highway

On a warm September morning, with the Pacific at my biker's boots, I headed out of San Francisco bound for LA. Separating the two metropolises was 450 miles of sublime coastal switchback, including a ninety-mile corniche of unsurpassable wildness and beauty. I couldn't stop grinning and beneath me was the reason why - a two tone "victory-red sunglow" Harley Softail Classic: 1340cc of unbelievable Kool.

Most of my round trip along America's first scenic artery would be restricted to single lane as the Hog and I burrowed through a string of towns as fabled as Samarkand: Santa Cruz, where the Beats had hung out and surfing was first taken up; chi-chi Monterey, the former sardine capital of the planet and immortalised by Steinbeck; chi-chi-er Carmel where squeaky-clean Doris Day had her animal sanctuary and Dirty Harry, aka Clint Eastwood, had been a mayor; and Santa Barbara, "home to the newly wed and nearly dead", which is about as chi-chi as chi-chi gets. But none of these, nor even San Simeon - the fantasy castle newspaper tycoon Randolph Hearst created - was the highlight of the tour. That honour goes to the road itself and in particular the slice that hugs the jagged coastline known as Big Sur.

Highway 1 opened in 1937. It took eighteen years to build, mainly because of the difficulty of taming Big Sur where the road coils like a python for those ninety miles. Here there are no shopping malls and no real towns - just four state parks, a concertina of bends and the most dramatic stretch of coastline in America. The road would be memorable even if you were driving it in a tank. On a Harley, it's simply sensational.

The bike plummeted and soared in and out of clifftop hairpins. The declivity was violent, weathered sandstone cliffs suddenly dropping 400 feet to serried bays of deepest indigo. Underground chasms drew in the sea-swell, creating the surge that made Big Sur *the* legend among surfers. At night the seascape was even more magical, the ocean taking on the waxy sheen of a whale as the moon turned everything else to silver and glass.

Of the four parks along its stretch, Point Lobos State Reserve ("the crown jewel of California's state park system") takes the biscuit. Here I abandoned the bike and walked the shore trail, watching sea otters floating on their backs in the kelp, and sumo-sized sea lions hauling themselves up onto rocks. With good reason landscape artist Francis McComas called the peninsula "the greatest meeting of land and water in the world". It impressed Robert Louis Stevenson sufficiently to serve as the model for *Treasure Island*.

The next day, I hiked for a couple of hours on the trails of Pfeiffer State Park and swam in its water holes. Once back in the saddle, I continued south through the serpentine coils of the corniche. It was easy to see why the writer and painter Henry Miller, like innumerable other artists, chose to live in Big Sur until his death in 1980. The houses in the densely wooded hills overlook knife-edge cliffs and an endless surf that fizzes up the coastline like a firecracker. At certain times of year blue and grey whales swim offshore with the dolphins.

Touring on a bike rather than in a car heightens the senses. The tarmac whizzed by just a couple of inches beneath my feet and with no one to talk to and no radio to switch on, there was nothing to distract me from a view that was neither pinched nor framed by a window.

Leaning in and out of bends splashed by sunlight beneath Gothic vaults of oak, sycamore and redwoods (some 350 feet tall and 2,000 years old) was as close to a religious experience as any biker's likely to get. On a bike you feel gravity, the fog, the wind and the heat. Then there are the smells - the tang of the acrid kelp floating on the ocean mixed with sage, jasmine, wild poppies and eucalyptus.

The other great thing about big motorbikes, and Harleys in particular, is that they are ice-breakers. Pull up, and within seconds someone will be snapping pictures and telling you about the Electra Glide they owned twenty years back.

At Santa Cruz, hotbed of university radicalism and the starting point for Ken Kesey's 1968 *Electric Kool-aid Acid Test*, I chatted to a local biker above the beach. Offshore a gaggle of surfers hovered like dragonflies, waiting to hitch lifts on incoming waves. One stood out: he was wearing a straw hat but still managing a headstand on his board as he surfed his wave.

Straw Hat's name, my fellow biker informed me, was Ed Guzman. "He's a biker too." Apparently Ed had been doing his headstands every afternoon for the past two decades. Later I spotted him playing his mouth harp further down the beach, facing the waves as the sun prepared to slip beneath the horizon.

Ed told me he'd been taught his headstand trick by the first person to accomplish this feat in America: his grandmother. Dorothy Becker Lineer in turn had been taught in 1915 by a Hawaiian named David Kahanamoku. Ed showed me a sepia-tinged photo of Grandma doing her thing at the turn of the century. Apparently she'd also been something of a wild dresser, a boxer and a world-record holder at the fifty-metre dash. Until her death in 1990, aged 89, she could still be seen regularly riding the Giant Dipper at the Santa Cruz fairground.

As I filled my tank at a gas station in Fernwood the next day, I got chatting to Eric Spencer, who was riding a '91 Softail Classic. Eric oozed Californian mild manners and melted vowels and fitted Harley's new Yuppie profile perfectly: inside the red bandana and biker's leathers was a 44-year-old attorney from LA. Earlier that year, he told me, his wife had "taken the home, taken the car, taken the money and the kids". A brief pause. "But I got the Harley."

Eric was returning from the Monterey Jazz Festival ("do it every year"). Having bonded as bikers do, we adjourned to the bar next door (the extent of ambition for settlements along Big Sur doesn't go beyond a gas station, a small post office and a bar). Inside, we soon struck up conversation with a holidaying Scottish couple who'd just been given a half-pound bag of marijuana by someone in a kilt they came upon in a cove playing a bagpipe to seals. Maybe. Maybe they were simply tripping.

Even weirder was my next encounter at nearby Big Sur Lodge in Pfeiffer State Park. Running the gift shop was Adana Simon, who, when she discovered I was English, decided I must be shown round the ancient forest by someone who was intimate with it.

After ten minutes we came to a bridge over a stream. This, she told me, was where she and her pitbull, Angel Butt, had come upon their first fairy. The fairy was "about four inches tall with large wings". Apparently she also had "a translucent aura and was a bit Mongolian looking".

A little further on, we arrived at the spot where Adana had had her first encounter, eighteen months earlier, with extra-terrestrials. Since that day she'd been studying hard with them. "I had been mourning the death of Angel Butt and had decided to leave Big Sur. I was walking through the woods here when *whooooooosh...*" Adana spun round and locked her arms by her sides. "The beam held me. I was being probed. I knew then I had to stay. I had a mission."

Her new friends measured five feet, were bald and came from Essassani in the fourth dimension of the star system Orion. We, too, apparently had all come from space and Adana's task was to assist in our evolution into a new species. Adana, I decided, had paid too many visits to the bagpipe player in the cove.

My own brain freeze moment on my Californian odyssey came when I foolishly exchanged two wheels for four.

Pismo Beach was the only section along the entire Pacific seaboard on which you could drive a car. Unfortunately, shortly after hiring a dune buggy, I found myself suspended in mid-air as I hurtled off a towering sand dune. Inexorably, the buggy's nose edged into a vertical descent and I smashed to the ground, my Harley helmet tilting backwards as my forehead crashed against the steering wheel. An ambulance ride and ten stitches later I was allowed to leave the Arroyo Grande Hospital. "We set 41 fractures one weekend off Pismo buggies," the registrar bragged, "And two died over the summer." Who said four wheels were safer than two?

With a zipper of stitches laced across my forehead and an impressive black eye, I felt in need of a little R&R and so booked in for a night at the San Ysidro Ranch in Santa Barbara. JFK and Jackie honeymooned here, and LA's stars and San Fran's successful writers still come to chill out in the plantation-style cottages that pepper the luxuriant gardens. As I was checking in, Yoko Ono was checking out.

ALASKAN LONELY HEARTS CLUB

As I lay back in my private whirlpool bath on the deck of my cottage, I took an hour and a half to drain a bottle of Napa Valley white, while straining to re-read through my virtually closed eye *Zen and the Art of Motorcycle Maintenance*. Very Zen. Above me towered the buff-coloured Santa Ynez Mountains. Sometimes life just feels right. The next day I drove into LA, turned round and did the whole thing again.